Grimoire of Wellness

Publisher
Balthazar Pagani

Graphic design and layout
Bebung

Editing
Fabia Brustia

The contents of this book result from research and studies undertaken by the author. Nonetheless, it should be remembered that, at the onset of persistent issues or symptoms, seeking medical advice to obtain an accurate diagnosis is recommended.

Vivida
Vivida® is a registered trademark property of White Star s.r.l.

Piazzale Luigi Cadorna, 6
20123 Milan, Italy
www.whitestar.it

Translation: Contextus S.r.l., Pavia (Christine Guthry)
Editing: Abby Young

ISBN 978-88-544-2186-8
1 2 3 4 5 6 30 29 28 27 26

Printed in China

ANASTASIA MOSTACCI

Grimoire of Wellness

Natural Wisdom for Body, Mind and Spirit

Illustrations by SARA MARCUZZI

Vivida

Contents

Principles of Reconnection

In your hands, you hold a grimoire, a book of magic.

This isn't a grimoire like those of the olden days, dating back between the end of the Middle Ages and the early 18th century, which were filled with records of angels and demons, and instructions on how to cast mysterious spells or make talismans or formulas to conjure supernatural entities. Nonetheless, it's a magic book and you will find a lot of magic in these pages, which will support you in reawakening that powerful spark dwelling within you. It's the magic of nature and the cycles of life; of sowing, growing and reaping the magic of descending inside of yourself and embracing the shadows to radiate more light; of the dance of opposites forever seeking harmony and beauty. It's the magic breath of life that inhabits you and that drenches everything in a single breath. This grimoire is a travel guide, a treasure map to facilitate your journey of immersion in nature, both inside and outside yourself, to awaken your feelings, to recall the secret language of the moon, the stars, the trees and the crystals, to reintegrate your divine and animal selves within you, your masculine and feminine powers, to reconnect to the cycles and reclaim what you may have forgotten, but keep inside, like a seed in a state of quiescence, ready to sprout and flourish. When I think of wellness, I think of connection first; we humans are part of the whole, our bodies are part of the earth's body, and we are the siblings of all visible and invisible beings that populate it, which is why feeling disconnected and isolated causes us to suffer and get ill. We're unfit for this!

Reconnection and getting back to feeling "at one" with the whole is a journey taken in baby steps that may last a lifetime, yet it will transform you from the very start. It's about reconnecting those threads that, as humans or as individuals, we severed and that are waiting for nothing less than to be reattached and intertwined with a new consciousness, creating a beautiful new tapestry. For me, writing this book was a journey of celebration in which to honor the path that has led me to feeling whole, connected and part of the sentient cosmos. It hasn't always been so; indeed, I can say it was a difficult and demanding journey, simultaneously necessary and salvific, a path studded with practices, intuitions, challenges, insights, deaths and rebirths. A journey where I was able to put together transformative tools and practices, visions and possibilities by traversing them one by one.

Looking back, I see the road I traveled; there was a time when I felt lost and disconnected, directionless.

There was a time when I didn't know the cycles and I could see no sense or direction along the path; I felt alone, randomly cast into an indecipherable world.

Now I see myself and feel at home even when times are difficult. I walk through a forest and feel amongst peers; I meet a doe and feel our hearts beating at the same rhythm; I know there's a time to sow and a time to flourish; I know that death is required to make new life possible. I move through the world without ever feeling alone, with the flowers singing their song when I'm open to listening, and the streaming water inviting me to flow, while the wind blows against my shoulders reminding me of invisible wings and lightness, and the fire guides me in the right direction where the heart burns. Feeling this alliance changes our way of being in the world; it reminds us that we are protected, guided and welcomed as we are at all times. It constantly brings us back to the realization that we are geared toward health and evolution, like everything else on this earth.

This grimoire is a path for a way to remember, consciously embodying the natural, evolutionary movement that is necessarily cyclical, alive and pulsating; the seed must be able to rest in the dark soil and produce deep roots to be able to grow. Growth takes time and flowering cannot be forced, just as the fruits grow and ripen when the time is right. And there's always a time for letting go, in which to descend into the inner self, a time for melancholy, nostalgia and sadness. There is a time for doing nothing, one for being. Although it's difficult to witness the end of things without attachment, and even if we'd like to always be in a productive and active state, nature teaches us that every moment must be respected, honored and enjoyed. That is the only way we'll bloom again, blossoming and finding the sweet fruit. That is the only way we'll live fully, embracing the other side of life.

Plants, animals, crystals and divine archetypes tell us about ourselves; these pure forms awaken the dormant, unknown or forgotten parts; their language sometimes is unintelligible, yet it just needs deciphering and it's there for us. As Baudelaire wrote in his poem *Correspondences*:

Nature's a temple where each living column,
At times, gives forth vague words. There Man advances;
Through forest-groves of symbols, strange and solemn,
Who follow him with their familiar glances.

The etymology of the word "grimoire" probably derives from Old French, in which *gramaire*, besides being a book of grammar, was also a book of the occult. This connection between grammar and the occult may appear strange, though it isn't at all, because it reminds us of the power of understanding verbal and non-verbal cues, body language, natural and invisible communication. Grammar is nothing more than an unveiling of the secret and internal rules of language; in the grimoire, in fact, we find a principle that helps us decipher life, the cosmos, nature and the central mystery at the heart of everything, including ourselves.

N
W
E
S

Traditionally, it was a journal filled with notes, spells and witches' recipes, often transcribed with abbreviations and cryptic annotations, so as to be inaccessible to most, and so that its wisdom and magic did not end up in the wrong hands. A magic book capable of evoking and re-evoking, of unveiling and unraveling mysteries, of conjuring allied forces and awakening secret correspondences hidden from the public. However, magic is everywhere, calling loudly from the core of the most intimate and mysterious of places in which it's kept: inside us.

Page after page, I invite you to go inside yourself, as you are a portal to everything, with an open curiosity and the charm of a child facing life confidently and feeling protected by big hands and broad shoulders. I invite you to rediscover the wonders of life, to reconnect the threads, to seek the bigger picture that is sometimes hidden. I invite you to feel with your body, with your emotions and your soul, to let yourself go through every practice, every suggestion and every recipe while always asking yourself whether it's appropriate for you and whether it nourishes you. I invite you to listen deeply and openly to yourself.

Why, yes, this grimoire is a map;
however, the compass is and always will be you.

CHAPTER 1

SOWING: The Roots of Wellness

When we think of the earth, we think of a fertile, somber place, of seeds stored in the dark so they can be nurtured and then sprout, of roots teeming underground, creating secret bonds between things. We think about the life cycles, the natural, seasonal changes that have their own rhythms, which extend to everything that's alive.

Sowing is an act of faith in what we cannot yet see, in the natural and cyclical phases that are often longer than we'd like, in the transformational power of everything that is dying into new life.

In this chapter, we'll explore how to reconnect to the earth with grounding exercises, listening to our ancestral roots, encountering the wisdom of trees and consciously using natural elements to nourish body and soul.

CHAPTER 1.1

RECONNECTING TO THE EARTH AND REDISCOVERING THE STRENGTH OF ONE'S ROOTS

Don't bring me cut flowers, even if they are immensely beautiful. I won't accept anything further, in my life, that has no roots.

(Ada Luz Márquez, Spanish educator, poet and emotionally focused therapist)

Chapter 1.1

Anchoring Oneself to the Present and Sowing Stability

In the morning, as soon as you awaken, spend some quiet time prior to diving into the hustle and bustle of daily life. While you are barefoot, imagine sinking invisible roots into the earth, like a sturdy, powerful tree drawing strength from the ground. Keep your eyes closed and focus on the rhythm of your breath: the air enters the lungs spreading calm and exits taking with it any tension or anxiety.

When you're ready, open your eyes and go into the bathroom before getting dressed. Get a ceramic bowl and fill it with lukewarm water. If you like, you may add a few drops of essential lavender oil to promote tranquility or rosemary to enhance mental clarity. Stroke the water with your fingertips to awaken your deeper self while visualizing any concerns melting into the bowl and gently evaporating.

Again, close your eyes and imagine being surrounded by a quiet forest at dawn; the morning light filters through the foliage and the fresh air caresses your skin. Each breath strengthens your connection to the earth and your inner balance. You sense the green energy of nearby plants flowing through you, as the smell of moss and resin envelop you.

Touch the sink with your wet hands, feeling its firmness and texture. The contact with water, the ceramic and your own body will give you back the sensation of a root safely sinking into the ground. Slowly open your eyes, breathing deeply and observing yourself in the mirror; in this calm and centered state, you are ready to face the day decisively and calmly. Now your every step will be taken in the knowledge of having deep inner roots that support you.

Chapter 1.1

The Body as a Landscape

Lie belly up on a mat or a blanket on the floor, arms slightly apart from the torso and palms facing upward, legs slightly apart and relaxed. If you notice your chin pointing too far toward the sky, place a flat pillow or a folded blanket under your head. Little by little, try to relax your body into the earth, sensing its support beneath you, feeling completely welcome, like in a mother's embrace.

Connect with your entire body, with the waves of breaths passing through it, the emotions and thoughts fluttering about, the inner and outer perceptions. Try not to add any thoughts or judgments, just allow yourself to observe what is there. When you feel your body relaxing, listen to your inner landscape; imagine your whole being like a scenery, with earth, sky, plants and animals. What is this landscape like? Observe its every detail, consider whether it's day or night, and your internal weather. What season is it in your inner landscape? Maybe it's spring, with its powers of rebirth and freshness, or perhaps summer, bright and full. Or it might be autumn instead, intense, colorful and deep, or winter, with its white calm, silence and darkness.

Observe everything with loving curiosity, as you would before a natural landscape that is unique and beautiful. By connecting with yourself like a place of the earth with its natural cycles, you'll be able to notice that every day the landscape changes, the seasons will change and you'll come to understand that you, too, are part of the body of the earth, which is forever passing through cyclical phases, because life itself is cyclical. Lovingly and respectfully feel welcome, as you are now, by yourself and the cosmos. Lovingly and respectfully feel yourself and the cosmos welcoming you as you are now.

Chapter 1.1

One Cannot Fly Without Roots

When we talk about roots, we mean the plants and trees that support and communicate with each other through them; it's the roots that create a community, by weaving connections between individuals and the land. As human beings, our roots are the ancestors, not only by blood, but understood as all the visible and invisible aspects that life assumed before incarnating in us. Our ancestors are the mountains, trees, plants, minerals, fungi and animals. Our ancestors are the myths, stories and elemental forces. Our ancestors are the whales, whose wonderful song contains ancient memories; our ancestor is the mycelial network that connects all of nature, conveying information and needs. Connecting with our ancestors is to embody a sense of wholeness with the cosmos to which we belong, no longer being separate from nature, but finding it within. To establish a relationship with your blood ancestors, you could collect their stories and photographs, cook family recipes or visit the places where they lived. Reconnecting with them will give you great strength, allowing you to feel resilient and supported; remember that, to come into the world, besides two parents you needed four grandparents, eight great-grandparents, 16 2nd great-grandparents, 32 3rd great-grandparents, 64 4th great-grandparents... Behind you there is an army of women and men who have let themselves be touched by love to give you the chance to be here, now!

If you can't find information about your family of origin, turn to a large, centuries-old tree, a mountain or a landscape from your childhood, and search for stories and myths that speak to your soul.

Always remember to express gratitude for what came before you, and don't forget that in order to flourish, you need well-fed, healthy roots.

Forgetting
one's ancestors
means being a stream
without a spring,
a tree without roots.

(Chinese proverb)

Chapter 1.1

Cooking Root Vegetables for Hearty Nourishment

Roots were among humans' first food resources and are the portion of the plant responsible for collecting nutrients from the soil; therefore, they are rich in minerals and vitamins as well as fiber and antioxidants. There are many edible roots and the range of their flavors varies from bitter to spicy and from sweet to salty.

While our ancestors' nutrition placed great emphasis on root vegetables, from the early Middle Ages, they began to be considered animal feed and food for the poor, being associated with states of penury and survival, where no other food was available. It was because of their underground origin that they were regarded as something lowly and obscure, unworthy of people of high rank, who were accustomed to eating foods of loftier origins.

This dichotomy between high and low, in which what is of value is always high, while the earth harbors something of little value, is part of a culture that has created a lot of separation among us and has disconnected us from our origins and our history as human beings. Actually, it's by consuming these very foods that we can mend this broken bond and return to feeling whole and grounded.

The edible roots are many and versatile; among the most common are carrots, turnips, beets and radishes; though parsnips, swedes, black oyster plants, horseradish, daikon, Jerusalem artichoke, cassava and lotus root are just as tasty.

In addition to these, the roots of medicinal plants are also excellent and beneficial, and they can support us with their healing properties.

To make them part of our daily lives, especially in winter when nature prompts us to rest and stay put, we can prepare a delicious, healing broth:

12 1/2 CUPS (3 LT) OF WATER – 1/3 CUP (30 G) OF DRIED CHIVES – 3 SHALLOTS OR SMALL ONIONS – 3 CARROTS – 3 CELERY STALKS – 1/4 CUP (20 G) OF DRIED BURDOCK ROOT – 1/4 CUP (20 G) OF DRIED DANDELION ROOT – A PIECE OF FRESH GINGER – A PIECE OF FRESH TURMERIC – SALT

Place all the ingredients into a pot and bring to a boil; lower the heat and simmer for at least an hour. This way, you'll obtain a broth with an intense flavor that will provide a sense of grounding, strength and connection.

Burdock Root

— ARCTIUM LAPPA

Native to Europe and Asia, this common plant grows in temperate regions and belongs to the Asteraceae *family.*

It has a tall stem, large leaves and purple flowers, though it's mainly the root (a taproot several feet in length) that is used in Western and Chinese medicine as a detoxifying remedy capable of cleansing the blood and detoxifying the liver, feeding the reproductive, immune and nervous systems, while also recommended for skin problems such as psoriasis, eczema and acne.

Its energy is grounding, nourishing and stabilizing. It strengthens and nourishes, helping us to get to the root of a problem and cleanse ourselves in depth. From a physical point of view, it has the ability to unburden us by assisting in the elimination of toxins and by rebalancing the metabolism; from an emotional point of view, it unblocks any emotional stagnation even if connected to a distant past. In this process, burdock root accompanies us with its stable energy and safe presence.

It can be prepared by infusing the fresh or dried roots overnight, or it can be used in soups, broths and mashed vegetables.

FOCUS

CHAPTER 1.2

GROUNDING PRACTICES AND EMOTIONAL STABILITY

To sow plants in a garden
means believing in tomorrow.
(Audrey Hepburn, British actress)

Chapter 1.2

Sentient, Anchored, Present

Grounding techniques promote being in the present moment, heightening awareness and helping regulate emotional triggers linked to stressors.

These simple exercises can help you calm down after a challenging event, bringing your nervous system back to a state of control, fostering a sense of physical and mental awareness and resetting that feeling of security that enables us to evolve and thrive.

Through the senses, they support your connection to your surroundings, leading you to regain confidence and balance.

Whether you are sitting or standing, always begin by noticing your support systems, given they provide direction and a sense of stability. Then attune yourself to the environment, as you maintain an expanded perception, capturing—besides what you see—smells, sounds, temperature and tactile sensations. Choose three stimuli that presently capture your attention, such as a little bird chirping outside the window, the scent of a vase of flowers, the soft, warm cat curled up in your lap.

Subsequently, focus on your inner self, noticing three more sensations, which may be physical, emotional, mental or thought related. For example, the breath passing through you, the saliva as you swallow, or your joyful mood. They really can be simple things; your only job is to notice them like you would landmarks when traveling along a new road; you're creating guideposts to help your nervous system self-regulate. This simple practice can be repeated several times a day, reconnecting you to the here and now every time.

Chapter 1.2

To Feel Light Like a Bee

Bhramari Pranayama, aka Humming Bee Breath, is based on the Sanskrit word* bhramara, *meaning "bumblebee." It's one of the pranayama techniques described in *Haṭhayoga Pradīpikā*, a classic Yoga manual written in the 15th century.

It entails a soothing breathing technique to stimulate the vagus nerve and activate the parasympathetic nervous system and help one become calm, relieving tension, anxiety and stress. To practice it, sit cross-legged or in a chair with the soles of your feet on the ground and your back straight. Start by observing your breath and gradually withdrawing your attention from the outer world, tuning into your inner self and giving yourself some time to attune to your inner changes.

Now move into Shahmukhi Mudra, the Seal of the Six Doors, by raising both hands to your face with your elbows at shoulder height, then use your thumbs to close your ears. Place the index fingers on your gently closed eyelids, the middle fingers on the nostrils by applying gentle pressure, the ring fingers on the upper lip exerting downward pressure, and the little fingers on the lower lip so as to close the mouth.

Now, with each breath, exhale by emitting a long and uninterrupted buzzing sound, experimenting with lower and higher tones and thus directing the vibration in the various parts of the body.

Repeat Bhramari Pranayama six times, then sit quietly and still, noticing its effects on you. You may follow up with another set of six repetitions, then do a third set of six.

No longer caught up in the vortex of thoughts, the past or the future, you will finally be able to settle in the presence of the heart.

“

The buzzing of the bees
is the voice of the garden.

(Elizabeth Lawrence, American actress)

”

Chapter 1.2

Honor Your Boundaries by Trusting Yourself

In order to establish healthy boundaries for yourself and in your relationships, start with deep inner listening. It's important to establish flexible personal boundaries and not to barricade oneself behind impenetrable, protective walls.

Boundaries are a vital part of relationships, and the inner work you will undertake to create them is fundamental; tune in to determine what you find unacceptable and against your values, where there may be room to open up to others and opportunities for personal development and growth. Consider boundaries as a way to improve relationships; by honoring those of another person, you will get to know them more closely and authentically, by honoring your own, you will know yourself better and gain more confidence in yourself. The plant world teaches us a great deal about this matter; look at a rose, as it blossoms it protects itself with its thorns! This is a reminder to keep our boundaries whole by balancing gentleness and a healthy discrimination between whom we welcome into our space and whom we don't. The yarrow teaches us integrity with its deep, strong roots remaining firmly planted in the ground. Compatible with hypersensitive people, it allows one to feel the full breadth of emotions without getting lost, while its healing properties demonstrate that any boundaries that were violated can be restored and that any wound can heal.

Nettle knows how to defend itself, yet it's also a sweet essence that can nourish and restore us through its richness in minerals and vitamins. It also acts on the immune system and guards the boundaries of our health.

1 cup of boiling water – 1 tsp of dried nettle
(or a few young leaves of fresh nettle) –
1 tsp of dried yarrow (or a flowering sprig of fresh yarrow) –
3–4 dried buds of Damask rose
(a handful of untreated rose petals and some thorns)

Prepare the herbal tea by soaking the herbs in boiling water and covering them. Let steep for 10 minutes. Strain and sip, meditating or writing on the subject of personal boundaries and relationships, while allowing these plants to guide you.

Chapter 1.2

Black Crystals, Ancient Root Keepers

When you hold a black crystal, its energy anchors you firmly to the present and helps you feel connected and balanced. These stones have the wonderful ability to absorb and transform intense emotions and negative vibrations and to clean the electromagnetic field; they are actual protective shields. Connected to the root chakra, which is all about grounding and stability, they help our system feel safe and relaxed.

These are crystals that have always had a special meaning in many traditional cultures; healers and shamans used them for protection rituals, to ward off evil spirits, as well as to communicate with benevolent guiding forces and our ancestors. They symbolize strength and resilience and have the ability to support us in encountering hidden parts of our psyche, guiding us through a deep inner journey.

Black tourmaline is a protective shield that protects against electromagnetic frequencies and psychic attacks; obsidian has the power to bring out the truth; while hematite is a black crystal with metallic reflections that provides deep grounding and protection, sustaining us with the energy of the earth. Black onyx connects mind, body and spirit, strengthening one's will and direction; shungite stimulates the immune system, increases the life force and harmonizes the spaces by purifying them; while black agate promotes courage and concentration. Meditating with black crystals can be a transformative experience. Hold a black crystal in your hand or, sitting with the soles of your feet touching each other, place it between your feet. Close your eyes, take some deep breaths and open yourself to receiving the energy of the crystal, feeling that you and it are both a valuable part of this planet.

Black Obsidian

Black obsidian is a volcanic glass known for its intense color and reflective surface. Since it solidifies quickly, its structure remains amorphous, thus, it cannot be considered a crystal as it's not characterized by an ordered structure. That's why it resonates with our unstructured and unconscious parts, bringing them back to the light, so they can be visible and transformed. It's a stone capable of absorbing intense energy, releasing difficult emotions embedded within us, resolving circular thoughts weighing on our system and trauma stored in our tissue. Considered a great healing stone, it's a staple in many folk medicine traditions: it can guide one through the dark parts of their psyche so one re-emerges with what was hidden in the shadows, one's gifts. Thanks to its properties, it will reflect one's true self, encouraging self-reflection and growth, teaching us to look at our wholeness with love.

Keep it with you at night because it's a stone that acts on dreams and works best when the ordinary consciousness is dormant.

Exactly because of its deep action, it needs to be cleansed often; immerse it in hot water and coarse salt and recharge it under the moonlight, avoiding eclipse days.

CHAPTER 1.3

CREATING SPACE FOR POSITIVE ENERGY AND HONING INTENTION

To become human,
one has to make space in oneself
for the wonders of the universe.

(Native South American saying)

Chapter 1.3

Nurture the Deep Yearning of the Heart

In the Yoga tradition, there's a way of planting the seed of transformation in consciousness, to be able to nurture it through practice and intention; that's the sankalpa method.

The word *kalpa* means "sincere desire"; *sankalpa* is not an ego-driven desire but expresses a deep will that connects us to the highest truth. Whatever you truly desire, whatever your soul needs to know and experience, it resides in your *sankalpa*.

You can contact and nurture it while you meditate, are deeply relaxed or during Yoga Nidra practices, when the brain is in alpha waves, a state of full receptivity, in which the mind is open to new information.

When you meditate or relax, take a moment to pause in the space of the heart, allowing a deep desire to emerge; it may take time, it may seem as nothing is happening, but through daily training to be in more expanded states of consciousness, the deep voice of the heart will reach you. When you have this voice clearly within you, try expressing it in concise and positive words, and in the present time. Some examples could be: "I am healthy in body and mind"; "I awaken to my authentic self"; "I am at peace." As well as: "Being of service with love"; "Generating magic"; "Creating abundance." To make your *sankalpa* effective and efficient, you must feel a burning desire to realize it, feeling it true within you and perceiving it with all your senses. As you declare it to the universe, the mind must be relaxed yet focused.

Start to live and act in your *sankalpa* immediately; include it in your practice, sustain it with your power and keep it to yourself, like a seed that must be kept safely inside the earth in order to sprout.

Chapter 1.3

Move as You Feel

In many sports and artistic disciplines, the mind imparts a command that the body executes. So, what happens when we make space to listen to the body? What happens is the body feels it can express its feelings, its wisdom, its needs; it feels it can trust that it will be heard. What happens is that we begin to build a new type of relationship with ourselves, which lays the foundation for a new sense of connectedness and more grounding in our presence. Every day you may give your body a little room to move spontaneously, maybe right after exercising, to balance your energy. Play some music that makes you feel good and connected, and spend a little time listening in stillness, then let the movement start spontaneously in your body and give yourself room, without concern for what you are doing or what you should be doing. You can start on all fours or even stand; notice how your body will seek out organic movements. Focus on your spine, visualizing it as a vibrant and sinuous snake; feel your whole body as something fluid, like a large drop of water.

Focus on your breath; allow it to reside in the whole body. If your body is tired, stop and rest, if it seeks the earth, give in to it, if it wants to find verticality, follow it. This might be difficult at first, but trust the body; it's like a caged animal being released and gradually finding its wild, instinctive nature. Awaken your instincts and somatic intelligence that is always alive. Little by little, this simple practice will turn into an important time to connect with yourself and the flow of life that inhabits you.

Fruits of the Sun, Positive Energy

Citrus fruits are the sun incarnated as a plant; their rounded shape, colored in the warm shades of yellow and orange, recall our star and speak to the element of fire. However, such characteristics don't just lead us to associate them with the bright center of our solar system. Besides their wonderful digestive, immunostimulant and purifying properties, as well as brightening the skin, citrus fruits are used in aromatherapy to promote a positive attitude and ease worries. Their essential oils help reduce stress, increase vitality and dynamism, and expand a sense of opportunity.

They are great allies in the wintertime, as they promote a positive mood and vitality when the production of serotonin and endorphins is decreased due to the absence of light. Sweet orange is energizing and invigorating, grapefruit acts on the mood and reinvigorates the body helping to eliminate toxins, bergamot is used specifically in skin care thanks to its purifying action. Lemon detoxifies and reduces stress and fatigue, mandarin is invigorating and promotes calm by relieving anxiety and supporting rest, lime provides mental clarity and focus, while petitgrain, extracted from the leaves and twigs of bitter orange, has a relaxing and calming effect on the nervous system.

For their antiseptic properties and their ability to lighten a space by elevating its energetic quality, citrus fruits can be used to clean rooms and household objects, causing your space and mood to be more vibrant, serene and open.

PEELS OF 3–4 ORGANIC CITRUS FRUITS (ORANGE, LEMON, MANDARIN, LIME, ETC.) – 1 CUP OF VINEGAR, EITHER WHITE WINE OR APPLE CIDER

EQUIPMENT: 1 GLASS JAR WITH AN AIRTIGHT LID – SOME MUSLIN CLOTH OR GAUZE FOR STRAINING

Fill the jar with the citrus peels and add the vinegar, close and let rest in a cool, dark place for one month. Strain the liquid through the gauze and transfer to a spray bottle. Shake well before use then spray directly onto washable surfaces and dry with a cloth.

Chapter 1.3

Prepare the Soil for Sowing

Nothing can sprout or blossom in a space that is too full, overrun with junk and energetically spent. Nature itself teaches us that the tree must let go of its leaves to make room for new buds, while the snake sheds its skin once it has become too tight. Emptiness is necessary for fertility; creating space is essential when we need to refresh and plant some new seeds. The home, the cupboards, the pantry, as well as the photo archives, our electronic chats and mailboxes are often cluttered and disorganized. Cleaning up and untangling ourselves from what is no longer practical and doesn't serve our growth will bring about cathartic change and emotional freedom, which will assist us in flowing more freely with life. The first big declutter will probably be the most impactful; following that, it could be appropriate to plan at least twice a year. As for material goods, concentrate on one room at a time, pick up each object and notice what it feels like, decide whether you want to keep it or if you can donate, sell or discard it. Observe the rooms of your home and try reorganizing them so they don't create any energetic bottlenecks and so there is a good flow. Most likely, memories and emotional experiences will be triggered by some objects; embrace them without fear and take a break if it all becomes too much.

As for digital decluttering: eliminate any excess files, unused apps, overflowing inboxes, ongoing and persistent notifications. You will reap immediate benefits.

Finally, consider doing a nice mental declutter as well by observing and reducing any negative self-talk, complaints and limiting beliefs, and making room for clarity and creativity.

A seed contains more
strength and power
than will be achieved
by the tree, and in you
there is the potential
of a latent spirit that is
much larger than
you might ever suspect.

(Rudolf Steiner, Austrian occultist,
esotericist and creator of anthroposophy)

Seeds

Seeds symbolize potential, survival and rebirth. They are the hope that a new beginning is always possible, they are the guardians of the cycles, of the beginning and the end, but they also teach us that the end is never final and that the death of something brings about the rebirth of something else. They are small and mysterious and contain a multitude of data; in each seed, there is a plant that has yet to manifest itself, though it's already there.

A seed can remain dormant for a long time, waiting for the right conditions to develop and thrive, and this is a great teaching: that everyone requires optimal conditions and loving care to evolve.

In his Acorn Theory, psychologist and philosopher James Hillman argued that each of us comes into the world with an innate image that defines them. Their uniqueness demands to be realized and expressed, just like an acorn exists to manifest into a majestic oak, and can never create a larch or a beech. Think of yourself as a seed with all the potential to express something extraordinary and perhaps dormant, awaiting the conditions to develop and thrive. What might these conditions be? How might you awaken your hidden potential and connect with your most authentic self?

CHAPTER 2

SPROUTING: The Cyclicality of Nature and the Body

Everything in nature is cyclical; everything follows the life-death-life cycle.

Cyclicality is all around us, simultaneously shaping and transforming every living thing. Even rocks undergo a cycle known as lithogenic, while water follows a hydrological one and winds move cyclically as well.

Day and night chase one another, the seasons come and go, and so the seed that grows roots turns into a blooming tree bearing fruit, which in turn will create new seeds and start a new cycle. Time is not linear, but cyclical; living in accordance with the natural rhythms will lead you to a more harmonious, simple and contented life. In this chapter, you'll discover the wheel of the year: how to eat according to the seasons, how to harmonize with the changes around you and how plants can support you through transitional stages.

CHAPTER 2.1

DISCOVERING THE RHYTHMS OF NATURE AND HOW THEY AFFECT OUR ENERGY

Secret correspondences tether nature's remotest parts, like the air on a summer's morning, pervaded by countless, fine threads going in every direction and exposed by the rays of the rising sun.

(Ralph Waldo Emerson, American philosopher, writer and poet)

Chapter 2.1

Discovering Cyclical Time

To tune into the natural cycles of seasons and changes, to be closer to a more sustainable routine for yourself and your life force, you may use planet earth as a model, the most expert guide there is.

Choose a place close to you that can be reached easily, without too much effort, and make a commitment to nurture a deep and intense relationship with this place. Just like you would with a person you like and are interested in, devote some of your time to the place, during which you'll also learn about yourself and feel good thanks to this relationship. Find a place outdoors that appeals to you and makes you happy; this could be a park, a forest or a riverbank. The important thing is that you plan to visit this spot at least once a month, twice is even better, visiting it consistently for at least a year.

When you go there, get ready as if you were meeting someone special, and note the landscape changing with the seasons. In winter it will be quieter and bare, but even before the start of spring, you'll feel the energy shift, you'll see more birds, hear more sounds, and slowly the buds will appear. Meeting after meeting, greenery will appear, flowers and animal life will become livelier and you'll see fruit appear that will gradually ripen under the sun. Summer will bring to fruition what will be ready to be harvested or discarded by autumn.

Observe the changing light and temperature, and always acknowledge what happens inside you: sensations, moods, thoughts. It will be a beautiful journey of harmonizing with life.

Chapter 2.1

Traversing the Wheel of the Year

The wheel of the year is a visual representation of cyclical time, and, although it's a modern construct, it refers to what our ancestors have always done, namely, celebrating the solstices and equinoxes.

The wheel is divided into four quadrants, each corresponding to a season, the middle of which is marked by a festive day occurring halfway between an equinox and a solstice, during which the intermediate energies are celebrated. During the winter solstice, the longest night of the year is commemorated as we entrust ourselves to the darkness and traverse it guided by our inner light. It's at this point of maximum decreasing power that the ascent begins, light gradually increases until Imbolc or Candelora, when the ice begins to melt and the animals emerge from hibernation. This expanding energy continues until Ostara, the spring equinox, a day when light and dark are in balance, and nature's rebirth is celebrated. The light continues to increase until Beltane, the festival of union and fertility, reaching its peak with the summer solstice, a festival to celebrate the sun's triumph on the longest day of the year. From here, the darkness begins to encroach imperceptibly, every day until Lughnasadh, the harvest festival. The autumn equinox is a time for cleansing and preparing ourselves to journey inward, beginning a new descent into our inner selves.

The mysterious powers of darkness summon us to Samhain, a time for reconnecting with our ancestors, letting what has run its course go, and preparing to face the darkest phase... before a new cycle begins.

"

The bird sings
not because it has a reason
but because it has a song.
Hundreds of flowers in spring
the harvest moon in autumn.
A cool breeze in summer
snow accompanying you in winter.
If you don't have a mind cluttered
with useless things, every season for you
is a good season.

(Zen poem)

"

Chapter 2.1

Wild and Cyclical Food

Our way of eating should always be in tune with the seasons, since the place where we live, the earth, provides us with whatever we need at any time of year.

The availability of all kinds of produce, specifically fruits and vegetables that may come from far away places with very different climates from ours, is something we shouldn't rely on. Even if we have the opportunity to eat tomatoes and bananas all year round and doing so occasionally isn't an issue, our diet should tune into local and seasonal food as much as possible. In fact, each season has a prevalence of one of the four elements, which may lead to an imbalance; nonetheless, the earth always provides us with the chance to restore our systems harmoniously with fruit, vegetables and native, seasonal plants. Such an example is rosehip, the berries of which ripen at the end of autumn and provide high levels of vitamin C, which sustains us during the colder months; or dandelion, which thrives in spring when the liver needs cleansing after a buildup over the winter period. Nature provides warmer, starchy foods in the cold season and water-rich, more refreshing foods from spring onward; following this cycle is what sustained our ancestors until now.

Industrial agriculture unfortunately reduces the nutritional value of our fruits, grains and vegetables, and because of the ecological overshoot, the soil is depleted of important nutrients; despite this, we can still depend on native foods growing abundantly and spontaneously around us to help us meet our seasonal quotas.

Chapter 2.1

An Herbal Tea at Dusk to Dance with Day and Night

The most obvious and common cycle is that of day and night, endlessly chasing one another in a perfect dance, flowing and transforming with the changing seasons. Inside us there's an internal clock, the circadian rhythm, governed by the hypothalamus: an area of the brain that regulates important functions such as hormonal production, digestion, body temperature and the sleep-wake cycle. If this function becomes dysregulated due to a hectic pace, shift work or excessive screen time, this can significantly impact one's sleep and mood.

To be more in tune, you could expose yourself to the morning sun for at least 15–30 minutes and try to manage your exposure to artificial light, specifically the blue light of electronic devices in the evenings, so that it won't affect your melatonin production. Sleep is not only needed for personal rest, but it's also a deeply sacred time linked to the environment, the cosmic cycles, the invisible, spiritual realm; prioritizing your sleep hygiene and harmonizing it with the day-night cycle will result in improved health of body, mind and soul.

Waking up and going to sleep at a regular time, as well as finding a few moments to rest throughout the day, will balance your circadian rhythm, while using certain plants to help relax your system can be greatly beneficial as well. Sipping an herbal tea as you begin to wind down and prepare for bed, with rituals such as a nice warm bath with relaxing essential oils (lavender or chamomile), journaling, reading or meditating, can be the prelude to a truly regenerative sleep.

3 TBSP OF HOPS – 2 TBSP OF LEMON BALM – 3 TBSP OF PASSIONFLOWER – 3 TBSP OF CHAMOMILE FLOWERS – 1 TBSP OF LAVENDER

Night-friendly herbal tea

Mix all the ingredients. Use a tablespoon of the mixture for 1 cup of boiling water, cover and let infuse for 10 minutes, strain and eventually add a little honey. You can store the mixture in a jar with an airtight lid.

Oats

— AVENA SATIVA

This annual plant, native to Northern Europe, is now widespread throughout the world, where it also thrives in arid soils, covering them in green stems that are several feet long and that turn golden in late summer.

The grains are of high nutritional value, but the green stems can also be chopped and used for infusions with remarkable properties. Rich in proteins, unsaturated fats, minerals and vitamins, it strengthens the heart and helps lower cholesterol, soothing the nervous system and promoting a state of inner peace that strengthens the body and energizes it. A great ally at times of stress, mental or physical pressures, it elevates the mood and increases vitality by raising the libido and balancing the hormones. Its soul is that of a colt running through a green field flooded in sunlight and swaying in the breeze; it provides us with the nourishment we require to live a full life without exhausting ourselves, giving us energy and reconnecting us to our surroundings, helping us open our hearts if we're a little closed off. To benefit from its properties, cook the oat grains and use them in salads or hot dishes, prepare a porridge with the soaked flakes and garnish with fresh fruit, or make an herbal tea by leaving the green stems to infuse overnight, to extract the maximal nutritional value.

CHAPTER 2.2

CELEBRATING THE LUNAR, SEASONAL AND PHYSIOLOGICAL CYCLES

Nature's most beautiful gift
is that it's a joy to look around and try
to understand what we see.

(Albert Einstein, Swiss American naturalized German physicist,
winner of the Nobel Prize in physics)

Chapter 2.2

Celebrating the Seasons by Creating Beauty

A seasonal table centerpiece is a lovely way to celebrate cyclicality and to bring a bit of nature and its qualities into your space. First, you'll need to select a large dish to use as support and place it in a designated spot, then you can choose a fabric to use as the base, perhaps changing the color every season or using a color that recalls the earth or grass. On the fabric, you may display stones or crystals, seasonal fruit, cotton to represent snow, some sand for summer and anything you collect outdoors.

The making of the centerpiece is based on the magic of observation; how nature changes around you and you finding small treasures to take home.

Stones, pinecones and sprigs of evergreen can celebrate winter, which you can pair with some spices like star anise, cloves, cinnamon sticks and maybe rosehip berries. In spring you could showcase colorful flowers like violets, primrose, iris and dandelions, cherry branches and maybe some feathers, hatched eggshells and other items collected on springtime walks. Ears of wheat, corn cobs, poppies, different types of shells and fragrant fruits could fill the summer altar, while in autumn you may choose chestnuts, pomegranates, pumpkins, mushrooms or leaves in warm and wonderful colors. Arrange each item with care, creating a small landscape that reflects the balance and complexity you observe in nature; this will be your way of giving thanks for the life and beauty of each season.

Chapter 2.2

Breathing the Cyclic Matrix

Our breath teaches us there must be balance in life, in our relationships, on earth, between giving and receiving. In every moment, the breath takes us back to this fundamental teaching: we cannot give without taking, we cannot become full without being empty, there is no expansion without contraction. Within us dwells a master of cyclicality: breath, the most intimate thing we have.

Breath is the very life that passes through us over 20,000 times a day, often, without us noticing; yet, if we try to be aware of it, we can learn that the breath has much to teach us. It can calm us, activate us, make us more present and energetic, let us experience the embodiment of cyclicality. Sit with your back straight or lie on your back and practice this breathing technique: inhale for 4 seconds, feeling the expanding movement of the rib cage as the air enters; hold your breath for 4 seconds, sensing this feeling of fullness that culminates with the desire to release the pressure; then exhale for 4 seconds, releasing and coming back to a vacuum; then keep your lungs empty for 4 seconds, experiencing how the peak of this vacuum gives rise to a desire to fill yourself with fresh air, anticipating a new cycle.

If you like, repeat this breath for a few cycles, gradually increasing the length of each phase (first it will be 5, then 6, then maybe 7 seconds), but never forcing yourself. As you go through these phases, which are like the seasons or like the phases of the moon, you will become more and more attuned to the cyclical matrix that pervades everything, feeling part of a movement that involves the entire cosmos.

In the breath, in an instant,
the living and the cosmos rejoin.

(Emanuele Coccia, Italian philosopher and author)

Chapter 2.2

Traveling with a Cyclical Diary

Keeping a diary to observe ourselves in relation to what is happening within and around us can be a beautiful journey of self-examination for a time or a life-long ritual that supports us; in any event, it's a useful tool for reconnection and awareness.

A cyclical diary considers the seasonal and lunar cycles, as well as our inner, hormonal cycles and how these changes affect our emotions, psyche and physiology. To better understand the cyclical patterns, begin by numbering the days from the new moon, or the first day of your period, continuing in ascending order until the next new moon or the first day of bleeding, when a new cycle starts with day one. In your journal, always note the season, the weather, the lunar phase in which you are and write down any changes you notice around you, like new buds on the trees, ice on the hood of the car, the flowering mimosa, the falling leaves...

If you are a woman of childbearing age, note what phase of your hormonal cycle you're in and describe how you feel overall, in terms of energy, mood, libido, appetite, mental focus, physical strength and what the dominant daily emotions are.

Write down dreams, physical changes, any symptoms and special events. You don't need to write much, though you're welcome to; the journal is a tool for self-examination, which after a few months should provide you with a lot of useful information, giving you a new perspective about yourself, while also helping you organize your life in harmony with the flow of cyclical energy.

Chapter 2.2

Cleansing with the Moon

In observing the moon's cyclic waxing and waning, our ancestors recognized its influence on the growth, life force, health and fertility of plants and animals. In its phases of expansion and regression, the moon affects the tides, our body fluids, emotions, hormones and births.

As it rotates around the earth, the moon begins to grow, a phase in which it's the best time to sow, both in an agricultural sense and in terms of one's projects and desires. In its fullness, the moon becomes a luminous disc that invites us to celebrate, discover and share.

Subsequently, its phase turns to waning and the moon gradually starts to hide, simultaneously leading us toward closure and prompting us to let go and cleanse ourselves.

The new moon is a time of renewal, of death and rebirth, in which to rid oneself of habits and emotional baggage, to restrict one's diet to allow the body to detoxify. It's a time to prioritize rest, calm and introspection.

In learning about these powers, and especially noticing their effects within you, you may feel like bolstering this natural cycle with a couple of days of purification during the waning moon and the new moon.

Restrict your diet by eating simply cooked vegetables and avoiding any type of hyper processed or fancy foods; not having to digest elaborate meals will allow your body to allocate more energy to cleansing itself naturally. You can support this process with an herbal tea that aids the cleansing work carried out by the kidneys and liver.

DANDELION LEAVES – HORSETAIL TOPS – BIRCH LEAVES

Black moon cleansing herbal tea

Boil 4 1/4 cups (1 l) of water, then add a spoonful of each plant, turn off the heat, cover and let rest for 10 minutes.

Once seeped, it's ready to drink. You can drink up to 8 1/2 cups (2 l) a day.

Tara

Tara is a figure found among both the Mahāvidyā (great sages) of the Tantric tradition and in Buddhism, and other forms of spirituality. The name literally translates as "star," while the Sanskrit root "tri" means "to traverse." Tara can guide us like the north star and helps us overcome challenges by making a happy resolution possible. Tibetans portray it in 21 shapes associated with different colors and attributes. Green Tara is the goddess of enlightened action, who takes us from fear to hope; she's called Ture, the Quick, because she rushes to the rescue as soon as she is called. White Tara, on the other hand, helps one achieve a long life, compassion and serenity. Red Tara draws the energy of attraction; yellow Tara attracts wisdom and wealth; blue Tara protects from enemies, and so on...

In its most esoteric version, it symbolizes the subtle energy underlying all phenomena that are conceived and dissipate within it, as well as the confidence that somehow helps us navigate endless change and uncertainty in the awareness that after daytime, night will follow, and after winter it will be spring again. Tara, who comes to our aid in dark times, reminds us that life is cyclical, that descending is necessary and that we'll soon rise up to the light again.

CHAPTER 2.3

RITUALS TO WELCOME AND EXPERIENCE CHANGE HARMONIOUSLY

The sacred is not in heaven nor far away,
it's all around us, and small rituals
can connect us to its presence.

(Alma Luz Villanueva, American poet and writer)

Chapter 2.3

Rites of Passage

Human life, like that of all living things, is cyclical, punctuated by circular rhythms and interspersed by transitions. These transitions, which in traditional societies are celebrated through rituals, are specific moments clearly marked by a before and an after, which provide clear awareness of what is left behind and what is beginning.

Witnessing and celebrating such moments can truly change the way we experience transitions, by imbuing them with awareness and acceptance, ushering in respect and self-love and, by extension, the possibility to share and celebrate with a community, which provides a richer and deeper meaning to life events.

It can be very different to experience certain transitions alone or with the support of loved ones, or someone who may have already gone through a similar event and can help find the necessary resources and tools. Experiences such as the menarche for girls, the semenarche for boys, pregnancy, abortion, childbirth, motherhood and fatherhood, menopause and andropause, the death of loved ones, old age, approaching one's death, as well as final exams, graduation, marriage and starting a new job, should all be experienced as significant rites of passage that can reveal great gifts, if we're prepared and supported in dealing with them and if we attribute them the right values.

We need to fully experience these transitions and process them, or else they become mere biological or social events. To the contrary, by acknowledging their evolutionary potential, we can reclaim the sacred in our daily lives, regaining the magic and intensity of life and assigning it a shared meaning.

Chapter 2.3

Closing a Cycle

Closing a cycle with a ritual is giving oneself space for love and healing and time for redemption, which brings us back to the path home to reap the rewards of what we have experienced. Through rituals, we can consciously process life's experiences by living and physically working through all the phases and initiations that existence brings our way, maintaining a deeply embedded inner timeline.

The transitions we ritualize are a space/time that is taken from a linear vision of time and transformed into a personal and collective ceremony marking a change of state.

Closing a cycle is a key step in processing what we have experienced, opening ourselves to something new and honoring the transformation that each experience brings. You may ritualize the closing of a cycle in the company of a select few or even by yourself.

Draw a warm bath using cleansing herbs such as sage, rosemary, rue or just some Epsom salts. Before getting in, discard your clothing by burning it or throwing it away, then get in the tub and give thanks for the cycle that has ended, what it taught you and how it helped you grow.

Step out of the aromatic bath and rinse off with a bowl of cold water in which you will have immersed blooms like rose, chamomile, mallow, marigold and mint leaves. Thoroughly dry yourself off, then wear a new outfit that you purchased for the occasion and that represents a new version of you. Nurture this new phase of life and this new you by eating something delicious and healthy, and by sharing it with your loved ones.

The ritual reaffirms
common patterns, values, joys,
shared risks, pains and changes
that bind together
a community. Rites connect
our ancestors and our
descendants, those who came
before us and those
who will come after us.

(Starhawk, American essayist, activist,
ecofeminist and theologian)

Chapter 2.3

A New Cycle Around the Sun

One of the most popular celebrations following us since birth is our birthday, when we celebrate being born and the start of a new cycle around the sun. The birthday originates from an ancient pagan custom that used to wish people well on the anniversary of their birth, for the purpose of protection and for blessing the year ahead.

The ancient Egyptians celebrated the emperor's coronation date every year by offering him delectable foods, while the Persians were the first to introduce the custom of a birthday cake. Likely influenced by such customs, on the sixth day of each month, the Greeks celebrated the goddess Artemis's birthday by preparing a white honey cake lit up by candles, which resembled the full moon, for the purpose of keeping evil spirits at bay. The lit candles on a cake, one for each year lived, have always had a special magical power, recalling the ancient sacred fires with which humans celebrated rites of passage. It's said that extinguishing them in one breath makes one's dreams come true, as the smoke rising to the sky takes them away. The cake coming out of the oven, a place of gestation and transformation, reminds us of the moment when we come out of the womb, while its round shape evokes the circularity of time and the completion of a cycle, thus representing the person celebrated and their good health.

4 1/2 cups (560 g) of flour – 1 1/4 cups (240 g) of sugar – 8 1/2 tbsp (120 g) butter at room temperature – 1/2 cup (160 g) of honey – 1 cup (240 ml) of milk (or non-dairy milk) – 4 eggs – 4 tsp of baking powder – 2 tsp of cinnamon (optional) – 1 tsp of natural vanilla (liquid extract or powder) – a pinch of salt

Preheat oven to 350°F (180 °C)

Goddess birthday cake

In a large bowl mix the flour, sugar, yeast, salt and cinnamon. Add the butter in pieces and mix until you get a grainy texture. Separately, combine the eggs, honey and vanilla, then add them to the previously prepared mixture by stirring quickly until you obtain a thick, creamy dough. Pour into a greased baking dish and bake for 25–30 minutes, checking if it's cooked with a skewer. Let cool, decorate with a sprinkle of powdered sugar and arrange the candles to celebrate your birthday.

Chapter 2.3

Learning How to Embrace the End from Mushrooms

The mushroom kingdom is a mysterious and immense place, a land between animal and plant life, a fascinating world that sometimes causes restlessness. Mushrooms live in the earth, the air, inside us; they can be minuscule but they are also among the largest living creatures on the planet. They have the ability to break down organic matter as well as stone or plastic, and they regenerate damaged ecosystems, affecting the atmospheric composition, neutralizing toxins and even reducing radiation, such as the fungus that appeared inside the Chernobyl reactor.

In popular culture, they have always been linked to magic and the supernatural, for their appearance and sudden growth and for the psychedelic effects of some species, used by shamans and healers in many areas of the world.

They can be healing and nourishing, but also harmful and lethal.

Their essence speaks to the relationship with nature, cooperation and collaboration; they reconnect us to the invisible network linking our body to the earth and our brain to the cosmos and the universe.

In nature their role is to transform and alchemize what is dead, inhabiting the places of decay, the deep darkness of the earth, the realms of dreams and visions. They teach us how life is reborn from death, how nothing is created and nothing is destroyed, but everything is transformed; if nothing dies, nothing can be born. In the life-death-life cycle, death is but a transition to another state that must be embraced and passed through as part of a continuous cycle, thanks also to the fungi, custodians of transformation.

Reishi

~ GANODERMA LUCIDUM

The reishi, aka "mushroom of immortality," is acknowledged as a spiritually powerful being with a long history of uses dating back to ancient China.

It was first discovered around 396 BC in the Changbai Mountains and was soon recognized as an important elixir of longevity. Given this wild mushroom's rarity, its use was restricted to the emperor and the Chinese nobility. In past traditional Chinese medicine, it was harvested and used in herbal teas or healing soups; nowadays it's widely grown for medicinal purposes.

With its shiny, waxy fruiting body, the reishi grows mainly on hardwood trunks, specifically oaks and chestnuts, and its color ranges from brick-red to purple and even black.

Monks and Taoist practitioners celebrated it as a Shen tonic, or soul-nourishing essence; it has immunomodulatory properties, rebalances the hormones and regulates various functions, as well as the central nervous, cardiovascular, digestive and endocrine systems. Its essence speaks to our spirit, prompting us to rest and regenerate, connecting us to the wisdom that allows us to evolve from a state of being reactive, in which wounds and learned patterns act, to a state of higher consciousness, capable of responding with grace and balance.

FOCUS

CHAPTER 3

BLOSSOMING: Energy and Vitality in Daily Life

Blossoming is a process that occurs spontaneously and cannot be forced. Once the soil has been prepared and the time is ripe and the conditions are favorable, blossoming takes place letting the uniqueness we nurtured bloom. We can't know when this will happen, we can't control it, but we can patiently nurture the seed and the shoot, making room to ultimately rely on life's process. Life wants to blossom, life wants to thrive and give of itself, of this one can be certain.

In this chapter, you'll learn to discard your old skin and renew yourself and your space, making it fertile and sacred; you'll learn to nurture being present and rely on plants to support your awakening. Finally, you'll experiment how to depend on the sun's and moon's energies to balance your inner opposites and ultimately bloom.

CHAPTER 3.1

ATTRACTING LIGHT AND ENERGY THROUGH RENEWAL PRACTICES

Go and let the stories, or life,
take place and work on these stories from your life,
shed your blood and tears over them
and your smile until they bloom, until you blossom.
(Clarissa Pinkola Estés, American writer, poet and psychoanalyst)

Chapter 3.1

Rejuvenate with Dry Brushing

Dry brushing is an ancient technique that, according to traditional Chinese medicine, helps our ability to adapt to change, both emotional and internal, as well as seasonal and climatic, supporting the flow of Qi, our life force. In Ayurveda, raw silk gloves were used to massage and exfoliate the body, stimulating lymphatic drainage and reducing fluid retention in the tissues.

In the mid-19th century, the German priest Sebastian Kneipp, hygienist and founder of hydrotherapy, introduced dry brushing as part of his therapeutic protocol, which aimed to strengthen the body by triggering the body's self-healing powers. This practice has great benefits: it promotes skin oxygenation and lymphatic drainage and makes our fascial system more flexible and functional, stimulating vitality; however, it should be avoided if you have dermatitis, psoriasis or other skin problems.

Use a special natural bristle brush and start from the feet, proceeding from the bottom upward, toward the heart, using small circular motions and counterclockwise movements on the ankles, calves, knees, thighs and buttocks. From the palms of your hands, move to the wrists using the same motion, gradually moving upward to the shoulders, rotating clockwise in the abdominal area to support peristalsis.

You can alternate circular movements with upward brushing. Use pressure that is appropriate to the body's various areas, taking care in the most sensitive ones and avoiding sensitive zones like the nipples. After dry brushing, shower or bathe, moisturizing your skin with a body oil or lotion.

Chapter 3.1

Refresh Your Energy with Floral Water

A hydrosol is a fragrant water made by distilling a plant; an aqueous portion is separated during the extraction of essential oils.

The therapeutic properties of the plant are transferred to the hydrosol in a less concentrated and more delicate ratio than an essential oil, which is why the product is safe for pregnant and breastfeeding women, children, elderly people and most pets.

Hydrosols make for excellent skin toners: helichrysum, calendula and rose soothe redness, being deeply refreshing and moisturizing; lemon balm and tea tree are advised for skin imperfections; mint and cucumber are cooling when it's hot; lavender and chamomile soothe minor burns. You may use rosemary on your hair to strengthen and prevent hair loss, as well as laurel, which is sebum-regulating and advised against dermatitis or dandruff. You can also use these floral waters for their aromatherapy properties, spraying them in rooms, on clothes and directly on yourself; choose citrus, mint and lemongrass to elevate and purify; rosemary and bay leaf to energize; chamomile and lavender to relax and help calm you; rose or neroli to create an atmosphere of sensual beauty.

The interesting thing is that, besides being readily available commercially, you can easily make your own hydrosols.

A moka pot – distilled water or spring water (to taste) – herbs, fruits or vegetables (to taste)

Get a rather large moka pot that you'll only use for herbs, given that coffee's strong aroma would alter the fragrances.

Fill the water tank with distilled or spring water, then fill the filter basket with your choice of plants, pressing them down. For this mixture, fresh and untreated plants are recommended, but you can also use fruits such as citrus or vegetables such as cucumbers.

Screw the moka pot shut and place it on the stove, following the usual coffee-making process. When it's ready, in the upper chamber you'll find your homemade hydrosol, which you can pour into a glass jar or spray bottle. Let it cool and store in the fridge for 1–2 weeks. Before use, always check it hasn't become cloudy or smells different.

Chapter 3.1

Create Your Home Altar

The main religions of the world see the altar as a "sacred table" for connecting with the spirit; traditionally, altars are in an elevated spot to celebrate religious rituals and make offerings to the gods. You may resolve to use a place in your home for this purpose, which will become the hub of your spiritual practice to express your gratitude and devotion to what you feel is meaningful. Before making the altar, select a room, then prepare it by thoroughly cleaning and tidying it, then cleansing it with incense or essential oils. Identify a spot that is central yet intimate, which can express your spiritual ideal and embody your heart's vocation.

As a base, you may use a brightly colored cloth to symbolize the power of life to enliven the altar and invigorate the spirit. Start with small objects that represent the power of the elements: a water-filled bowl or a shell to symbolize water; crystals, stones, seeds or seedlings for the earth; a natural candle for fire; feathers and incense for air; eventually flowers or bells for the ether. You may add figurines or devotional images meaningful to you, trinkets you consider sacred and precious. Set up the altar as a small, balanced and orderly world that expresses what you want to develop within you. But above all, keep it activated, clean and dust-free, fragrant and cared for; use it as a space for contemplation, meditation and prayer, but also as a place for offerings and to express gratitude, and it will become the beating heart of your home.

We are born within
and through the earth.
Simply put, we are terrestrial.
The earth is our origin, our
nourishment, our teacher, our
healer, our realization.
After all, even our spirituality
originates from the earth.
The human being and the earth are
totally entwined in one another.
Without spirituality on earth, there can
be no spirituality in ourselves.

(Thomas Berry, American thinker, historian,
religious scholar and Catholic priest)

Chapter 3.1

Incense Burning for Energy Renewal

Since ancient times, in the East, specifically in India and Japan, the custom of burning incense has been used in religious rituals. In Native American indigenous cultures, we also find the burning of incense and herbs, especially white sage, as well as sweetgrass, cedar and tobacco.

In shamanic culture, smoke has a very important purpose: it's a vehicle to communicate with the spirit world; it purifies a space, promoting healing and causing a kind of trance in shamans.

In the West, we find this practice in ancient Greece, especially in churches, besides hospitals and clinics, to create an atmosphere that's conducive to prayer and to purify the space, the faithful and the pilgrims. Well-known are resins such as frankincense, myrrh and copal, whose smoke is highly purifying and induces a state of well-being. Although today we are increasingly looking for exotic plants such as palo santo, white sage or sandalwood, which for this reason have become endangered species, it's worth rediscovering simple and local plants, widely spread but equally powerful. Laurel is a valuable protective herb, sage provides energy, lavender disinfects and relaxes, rosemary and thyme are powerful antibacterials, mugwort strengthens the psyche and heightens intuition, lemon balm promotes calm and joy, Helichrysum clears the lungs and brightens vision, and you can collect the resin of conifers while walking outdoors. Create your smudge stick by tying together the herbs you selected or make a mixture to be burned on charcoal, blending dried plants and resins in a mortar. Burn your plants when you feel like revitalizing the energy and cleansing yourself of burdens and negativity.

The Snake

The snake brings with it the medicine of renewal, intuition and the art of shedding old skin. It moves sinuously while connected to the earth, whispering secrets to those who are sensitive to the vibrations and intertwining with the lineage of priestesses and oracles linked to the civilization of the Great Mother. It guides us to listen to what is hidden, connecting us to the life-death-life cycle and the capacity to heal and renew. The snake teaches us that transformation doesn't mean turning into someone new, but returning to the origin and essence of who we are, which has always been there, under the layers of conditioning and old histories. It teaches us not to resist transformation and be confident that life will get us to where we need to be, nurturing the wonderful vulnerability that manifests at times of change. As it changes skin, its eyes blur, it enters a trance-like state and begins to wriggle, rubbing against trees and rocks to help the old skin break away. It gets rid of what is too tight, surrendering without holding back to be reborn in a new skin as delicate and sensitive as the dawn of a new day.

CHAPTER 3.2

MEDITATIONS TO AWAKEN THE INNER SELF

The earth knows you,
even when you feel lost.

(Robin Wall Kimmerer, Potawatomi forestry biologist, academic and writer)

Chapter 3.2

Immerse Yourself in the Moment, Experience the Wonder

The state of being present is defined by pure and simple perception, not necessarily without thoughts or emotions, but rather, without attachment or identification with them. One simply observes what is happening in a neutral way.

It may seem like something complex to achieve, given that for many of us, the state of mind is that of a "crazy monkey bitten by a tarantula"—as they say in Yoga—in reality, it's a natural and spontaneous state that is easily recognizable in animals.

Recall a time when you had an intense experience, maybe before the magnificent colors of a sunset, encountering a wild animal in nature, contemplating an artwork... Remember how you were totally unified with the experience. The mind is a wonderful tool when used appropriately, yet it's never in the present; it's always in the past, comparing experiences, or in the future, trying to predict or control what will happen. When you are present, however, you are able to live the experience and immerse yourself in pure perception.

You can train yourself to practice being present by paying close attention to what you are doing, like washing dishes. Focus all your attention on your body, your breath and the action you are performing; the movement of your hands, the feeling of water on your skin, its sound, the consistency of the sponge, the smell of detergent and the foam that is created. As soon as the mind wanders, gently lead it back to the here and now every time. Incorporate more opportunities to be present in your daily life; to awaken presence is to awaken your spontaneous, wild and infinite side and fully enjoy the wonder of this moment.

Chapter 3.2

Practices to Support Inner Awakening

In his writings, Bulgarian philosopher and pedagogue Omraam Mikhaël Aïvanhov devoted himself to the inner transformation of the individual in balance with the laws of the divine world, through simple and profound awakening practices that we can draw inspiration from in our daily lives.

He advises to wake up before dawn and contemplate the rising sun, looking at it as an ideal to be followed with devotion every day; by learning from the sun how to give and love unconditionally, we near our higher self. Whenever we see a tree, let us look at it as a living being, greeting and honoring it to connect with the life circulating from the roots to the top of the branches, accepting it and opening ourselves to its power and connection. Laughing should be considered a spiritual practice: it lightens the soul, nourishes the brain, connects us to others, opens in us the spring of life, positivity and joy. Let's learn to laugh more, alone and with others.

Music is also a medicine that carries us into a new world, and it's a powerful ally to our awakening. It's a universal force that's present in all of nature, an expression of the cosmic rhythm. Music and singing are manifestations of the heart, capable of reflecting the universe's harmony. Preparing food with love and blessing it with words that we feel are sincere, and thanking the earth that sustains us, can change our perspective on food and the way we eat, while also improving our digestion.

Finally, before going to sleep, let us sow joyful thoughts and hope that can be nurtured overnight, to help us rest well and meet the new day with an open heart.

Chapter 3.2

Plants for Awakening

Plants are our teachers and can really lead us on a personal and collective evolutionary journey; if we are willing to listen to them and let them guide us, they will reveal their gifts to us and support our spiritual awakening. There are many plants that are considered teachers, such as the entheogenic plants used in shamanic traditions. Every plant, even the humblest, can teach us a lot and improve our awareness through its qualities, from the most physical to the most subtle, helping us be present as life passes through us and frees us from limiting thoughts and acquired patterns.

For example, *Centella asiatica*, aka Indian pennywort, in the culture of Northern India is considered an herb that promotes subtle awareness and spiritual advancement. It's a plant that elevates the psyche and heightens intuition, favoring a state of brain waves in the alpha, gamma and theta spectrum, associated with expanding consciousness and meditative states.

Ginkgo biloba, used as long as 5,000 years ago as an elixir of life in the imperial court of ancient China, is one of the oldest remedies known to mankind and promotes the microcirculation of the nervous system. It seems that in the past, Taoist monks and practitioners carved their spells and symbols on ginkgo wood to access the spirit world.

Lavender is well known for its scent, but perhaps not everyone knows that it's calming and soothing, and that it resonates with the sixth chakra located between the eyebrows, a point of foresight, intuition and enlightenment. It's ideal for anyone who always feels stressed, promoting a deeper and more intuitive spiritual understanding.

2 PARTS CENTELLA ASIATICA – 2 PARTS GINKGO BILOBA –
1 PART LAVENDER

Prepare your blend by mixing the ingredients.

Boil a liter of water, pour in a handful of the mixture, turn off the heat, cover and let infuse for 10 minutes.

Strain and drink throughout the day, in between meals.

Chapter 3.2

Mother Earth, Father Sky and the Zone of Presence

This simple practice will help you experience firsthand the vitality and universal intelligence that inhabits you by dissolving the mind/body dichotomy, allowing you to rest in a zone that will energize and guide you. Sit cross-legged on the floor or in a chair with the soles of your feet flat on the ground and your back straight. Feel the support beneath you coming from the earth; feel its stability, solidity and the support it's giving you by allowing you to lean on it. Take time to appreciate this connection, feeling that with each exhalation you can lean in a bit more. If you feel a lot of movement inside you, try stretching out the exhalation a bit more to help your system slow down and adjust. Then, as you inhale, follow your midline to the top of your head and open your perception to what is above you: the sky, with its lightness and luminous spaciousness and its sense of possibility. Tap into it and open yourself to its vastness.

Now you are connected to Mother Earth and Father Sky through your midline, which is a place of vertical union, and you can also open up to the horizontal plane by individually perceiving: the back of your body, the front, the right side and the left side. Once you have felt them, you can imagine widening them and creating a sense of expansion and radiance, like a bubble extending from you. Finally, center your heart, feel its presence in your chest, its warmth, like a flame burning at the center of you. Keep focusing on the heart and open yourself to feeling your present experience.

Observe yourself: you have in you heaven and earth.

(Hildegard of Bingen,
German Benedictine abbess, writer,
mystic and theologian)

Tulsí

— OCIMUM TENUIFLORUM

Tulsi, aka sacred basil, is highly revered in Ayurvedic medicine as an adaptogenic remedy that helps the body adapt to what it's experiencing. It has been widely used to aid digestion, soothe the nervous system and the adrenal glands, and to reduce inflammation; it's considered a cleanser of mind, body and spirit.

Its properties are warming, purifying and regenerating. Tulsi occupies a special place in Hindu courtyards across India, where it's planted for its auspicious powers and its protective and restorative nature. The very name "tulsi," which means "the incomparable," has a radiant and purifying vibration that nourishes the mind, body and spirit. It can be used as an essential oil and diffused in a space to promote vitality, or used as a herbal tea or as an aromatic herb in the kitchen. Its scent is herbaceous and reminiscent of fresh basil and mint, with warm and spicy top notes.

In ancient Vedic texts it was considered an incarnation of Lakshmi, the goddess of abundance and prosperity, embodying paradise on earth and nature's abundance.

CHAPTER 3.3

THE POWER OF THE SUN AND MOON TO STRENGTHEN BODY AND SOUL

And wherever I go, there I shall always find the sun, the moon and stars; I shall find dreams and omens, and converse with the gods!

(Epictetus, Greek Stoic philosopher)

Chapter 3.3

The Sun and Moon Orchestrate the Cosmic and Physiological Cycles

The cycles of the sun and moon are inscribed in our physiology in a profound way; the male and female hormonal cycles are designed with an imprint of the cosmic rhythms. The woman's hormonal cycles are a wonderful dance choreographed by hormones such as estrogen and progesterone, which manifests with menstruation, the central event of which is ovulation. Just like the waxing and waning of the moon, the female cycle equally presents a phase of growth culminating in that moment of fullness that is ovulation, in which the creative powers are at their peak. This is followed by an actual decreasing phase, in which in the absence of conception, the inner lining of the uterus, which was ready for the possibility of pregnancy, disintegrates alongside the egg and is eliminated through the menstrual blood; this is a moment of release that can be compared to the new moon, when everything is dark and quiet. The male hormonal cycle is mainly linked to the hormone testosterone and, unlike the female cycle, follows a distinct rhythm inside each individual day. That's why male energy appears more linear and constant. The testosterone cycle is linked to the solar one: at dawn the testosterone level is highest, reaching its apex around midday when the sun reaches its zenith, then its production drops in the afternoon, reaching its lowest level at night.

The male cycle is also linked to seasonal changes, as testosterone levels are also subject to daylight hours and actual time spent outdoors. Sun and moon are inside us, guiding us through the most powerful manifestations of life: sexuality and the ability to create life.

Chapter 3.3

Breathing the Sun and Moon

The Yoga tradition teaches us that there are two important energy channels in the body called Ida and Pingala; one is connected to lunar energy and the other to solar energy.

Developing a connection with lunar energy allows you to feel fresh, calm and nourished. It may help you develop your intuition, feel rooted and invigorated; additionally, its lenitive qualities promote sleep and ameliorate stress levels. You can practice by focusing on your exhalations, extending them and breathing continuously through the left nostril (blocking the right one), where Ida nadi comes to a head. The energy of the sun brings enthusiasm, inspiration and a sense of purpose. You can practice by focusing on inhaling and breathing through your right nostril, to strengthen the connection with Pingala nadi, the solar channel culminating in this nostril. Nadi shodana is a breath, the purpose of which is to balance these two forces within you and to purify all the nadis, or energy channels, which in the subtle physiology of Yoga, are said to be 72,000.

Choose a comfortable position that allows you to keep your spine elongated without causing tension, then rest the index and middle fingers of your right hand in the middle of your eyebrows, and alternate closing one nostril at a time. Cover the right nostril with the thumb to inhale slowly from the left; then cover the left nostril with the ring and little finger to exhale from the right, and reverse, inhaling from the right nostril and exhaling from the left nostril. Repeat this cycle alternating several times, keeping the inhalation time equal to that of the exhalation. Keep your eyes closed and visualize the path of the air flowing through you, with the energy of the sun and moon.

Chapter 3.3

Dancing in Harmony

The sun is connected to our ability to act, think, speak and move in the physical world; while the moon represents the most intuitive part that is open to the universe's intelligence, understanding, acceptance, the ability to alchemize and transform. Both of these forces exist in all of us, in unique combinations and constant flows that endlessly redesign their equilibriums. Our lives often have hectic schedules and are strongly unbalanced toward action; our minds are often overactive and even when we move our bodies, we tend toward a more solar energy. On the other hand, there are practices that have a more lunar energy and can help us regain inner awareness, calm, presence and intuition. Learning to balance one's energy is a refined art that first off requires listening to our body, when oftentimes we tend to be more demanding of it.

What you can do is start from the body itself; begin by moving intuitively, maybe standing or crouching, feel where the body wants to go, feel what energies are present and which ones you want to give in to, acknowledging rather than suppressing what is present in you now. Maybe there's a lot of energy and you have the whole day ahead of you, the sun is high and your body demands some vigorous exercise like a run, or maybe you're tired and need to recuperate with more gentle movements and stationary poses, or you want to declutter your mind and relax your body before going to sleep, releasing tension and opening yourself to the spiritual dimension of dreams. Start listening to yourself, your body and your mind, manifest the sun and the moon, and begin to dance.

"The heart of a human being
is no different than the soul of heaven
and earth. In your practice always
keep in your thoughts the interaction
between heaven and earth, water and fire,
yin and yang."

(Morihei Ueshiba, Japanese martial artist
and founder of aikido)

Chapter 3.3

The Extractive Powers of the Moon and Sun

Did you know you can use the powers of the sun and the moon to extract the active ingredients and beneficial properties of plants?

Thus, you'll not only be able to create your own delicious and powerful infusions, but you'll also have them charged by the powers of our "central fire" (as defined by poet Mariangela Gualtieri), and the fascinating queen of the night. You can prepare a lunar infusion by leaving a transparent container with plants immersed in boiling water overnight, beneath the moon's rays, which will thus absorb the spiritual and intuitive qualities related to the occult properties of the moon.

The lunar infusion will have calming and lenitive qualities, and will stimulate intuition; plants related to women's health such as mugwort, the moon plant par excellence, are recommended as well as green oat, lemon balm, rose, blue lotus and lavender. You can also experiment with other plants you know, noting how the effects of the potion change by exposing it during the various phases of the moon. With the solar infusion, leave the container in direct sunlight for several hours, so that the plants absorb energy and heat, increasing their warming, bright and activating qualities; this potion will provide strength and energy, and is suitable for plants such as calendula, rosemary, lemon verbena, rosehip, citrus fruit and nettle, though you can experiment with your favorite plants, too.

For these blends, you can use fresh herbs, which are more powerful due to their heightened life force, but remember you'll need about twice the amount of dried herbs.

MUGWORT — LEMON BALM — DAMASK ROSE

Fill a 2-cup jar with the following: 4–5 dried buds of Damask rose (or the fresh petals of an organic rose), 6–7 lemon balm leaves and the stem of common mugwort. Pour boiling water into the jar, then cover the opening with a piece of gauze that you'll keep in place using a rubber band to prevent anything from getting into the brew. Leave the herbal tea directly under the moonlight all night. Strain and sip, paying close attention to the reactions, thoughts, emotions and sensations that come your way.

Amaterasu

This sun goddess is considered the source of all the world's energy and vitality. For centuries, she's been revered in Japan, where she's considered the ancestor of the imperial family. Her name literally means "The Great Goddess Who Shines in Heaven," and she embodies values such as justice, wisdom, prosperity and protection. Her role in Japanese myths and legends emphasizes the importance of light, harmony and the preservation of life. As the goddess of the sun, Amaterasu represents not only the life force that fills the world with light but is also a symbol of rebirth and hope. Legend has it that Amaterasu retreated into a celestial cave following a dispute with her brother, Susanoo, the god of storms, plunging the world into darkness and causing catastrophes and despair. Worried, all the gods gathered outside the cave to try and get her out, so they decided to put a mirror before the cave and ask the goddess of dawn, Uzume, to perform a dance. Uzume's dance became more and more unbridled causing great laughter, which drew the sun goddess out of the cave. In seeing her own reflection, she approached the mirror struck by her own beauty, while the door to the cave was shut behind her and she once again illuminated the world.

CHAPTER 4

BEARING FRUIT: The Harmony of the Elements

Fruit comes as a blessing, yet it's the result of everything you have sown, grown and let blossom. Fruit is the gift, the fullness, the sweetness that allows you to look at the journey from a new perspective. When you taste fruit, you are nourished by a story unfolding in time, a process of growth and transformation, a being that has already experienced a whole series of developments. It's time to celebrate, to enjoy what you can harvest and savor. Above all, it's time for gratitude.

In this chapter, you'll learn simple exercises, rituals and nurturing practices to integrate the power of the elements and to harmonize and align yourself with the cosmic forces, making alliances to support your journey on earth with a holistic outlook, in which the relationship is always central.

CHAPTER 4.1

INTEGRATING EARTH, AIR, WATER AND FIRE IN EVERYDAY LIFE

Earth, my body
Water, my blood
Air, my breath
And fire, my spirit

("The Four Elements" by Peter Vadhar, Mexican musician and producer)

Chapter 4.1

Purifying Emotions with Water Medicine

Water speaks to emotions, fluidity, creativity, the origin of life and memory. Water reminds us to flow and that stagnation leads to decay and reduced life force.

Emotional energy needs to flow like the water of a river; instead, we oftentimes cling to emotions and suppress them, we identify with them, load them with judgment and mental regrets. When you feel stagnant and emotionally burdened, you may turn to water medicine and purifying practices using steam.

Countless traditions around the world use sweat as a cleansing practice, such as the Native American's Inípi, South America's Temescal, Northern Europe's saunas or the Turkish baths. These rituals act as physical and emotional purification practices because they help release stagnant or stored emotional water through bodily fluids.

You can create your own sweat lodge at home to cleanse your internal water using a pair of thick, fairly large blankets and a saucepan. Boil the water and then add a couple of handfuls of herbs in tune with the water spirits, such as horsetail, blue lotus or rose. Cover and let infuse for 10 minutes. Place the saucepan on the ground, remove the lid, undress and kneel before the saucepan; you may place a pillow beneath your knees to be more comfortable. Cover yourself completely with the blankets to retain the steam inside your small personal tent. Take your time to sweat, inhale the vapor, express your emotions, sing and even shed a tear. Let everything that is stagnant in you begin to flow again.

Chapter 4.1

Grounded Like a Plant

An oleolite (aka medicinal oil) is a vegetable oil in which plants and flowers are macerated to extract their fat-soluble properties.

The use of oleolites to moisturize and massage the body has a nourishing effect on the skin and a calming one on the nervous system, helping us unwind and combat stress. From an Ayurvedic standpoint, it removes an excess of Vata from the joints and mind (anxiety, worries, insomnia). Furthermore, a medicinal oil massage improves the immune system, helps us heal and strengthens us.

Yarrow is a plant that stands upright and has strong, deep roots in the soil; it speaks to boundaries and protection. In fact, it has hemostatic properties, assisting the healing of physical and emotional wounds and helping overcome defensive mechanisms that sometimes turn against us; it also supports our integrity in relationships.

It's a plant that will help you ground yourself and work on your boundaries, integrating the element of earth, a spirit that will help you nurture your sense of belonging to planet earth's body.

A VEGETABLE OIL OF YOUR CHOICE (GRAPESEED, SWEET ALMOND, COCONUT, SESAME, APRICOT KERNEL, EXTRA VIRGIN OLIVE OIL...) – YARROW FLOWERS AND LEAVES – A CLEAN GLASS JAR

You may prepare the oil with either dried or fresh flowers and leaves; in this case, leave them in the open air (but not in the direct sun) for at least 12 hours, so they may lose some of their moisture. Place the yarrow in the jar until it's full, without squashing it, then fill it to the brim with the oil, close and place away from direct sunlight for a lunation. Once ready, strain the oil using a gauze or a drip coffee bag and store in a dark glass bottle, away from sunlight, which would cause it to spoil faster.

The oleolite can also be prepared by heating the oil and plants in a water bath for at least 60 minutes, ensuring the oil never reaches boiling point, then it's strained and stored as above. Use this oil to massage, moisturize the skin and heal small wounds and abrasions, to feel grounded, present and whole.

Chapter 4.1

Dancing in the Wind

The element of air links us to lightness, speed, breath and vitality. It's everywhere and it's formless; through the breath, it connects us to all living beings and simultaneously finds its home inside our chest and the place of the heart, reminding us that being in an active relationship with the other and what surrounds us are vital.

It's the element connected to speed, ideas and new beginnings; it's invisible, yet it interacts with us through movement, like the wind moving things. It is linked to our ancestors, those who came before us and who guide us from the invisible.

In the body it's connected to the lungs and skin, the arms and hands, which are the wings of the heart. It expresses itself through touch, the sense that speaks to relationships the most.

To connect to the element of air, choose an elevated place like the top of a hill or a mountain, though a city balcony is just as good. The experience will be even more powerful on a windy day. From this vantage point, observe how the air moves the leaves of the trees and interacts with the flight of birds and insects. Connect with your breath by noticing how you are constantly traversed by the breath of life, then focus on your skin and the parts of the body that are exposed, welcoming the feeling of the wind caressing you and all the other sensations it provides. Finally, let the wind move you as if you were a hovering leaf; start with small movements in the fingers, hands and wrists, letting the body respond to the air's caress, explore the qualities of lightness and expansion, allowing the movement to involve the whole body. The breath traverses you, the wind moves you, the air invites you to dance, and you discover yourself to be light and vital.

Chapter 4.1

Be the Flame

Trataka, which in Sanskrit means "staring," is a cleansing practice for the sight and the eyes, specifically, the eyeball and optic nerve. Sight is the sense connected to the fire element, which brings direction and elevation, purifying and burning, transforming and alchemizing what passes through it. To practice trataka, get a candle and place it at eye level, so as not to strain your neck muscles; practice sitting with your back straight and shoulders relaxed, the soles of your feet or the ischia well grounded, depending on whether you are seated or on the floor. Keep your gaze fixed on the flame with awareness and focus, trying not to blink, and continuing to breathe while being relaxed. Focus on absorbing the flame through your eyes.

Soon your eyes will begin to tear up, providing your gaze with a good cleanse. Thus, close your eyes and visualize the flame internally, until it fades from your vision. Then open your eyes and practice fixing your eyes on the flame again, as if you could drink it in with your eyes, until the cleansing tears return.

Repeat for a total of about 5–10 minutes, feeling comfortable throughout and gradually increasing the time.

This is a practice you can do every day as it promotes eye health, increasing visual capacity, strengthening the optic nerve and improving concentration. While you practice, feel how the fire nourishes, transforms and strengthens you, helping you achieve a clear vision and supporting your purpose, like an arrow shot by an archer.

“

The one advantage
of playing with fire is that
no one ever gets singed.
Only those who
don't know how to play
with fire get singed.

(Oscar Wilde,
Irish writer and playwright)

”

Clear Quartz

Aka hyaline quartz, this crystal assists in integrating the powers of all the elements, amplifying the effects of our practice and heightening our intuition. As part of the quartz family, its trigonal structure promotes balance and allows the channeling of light. One of the main balancing features of crystals is their geometric structure, since it resonates with our own structure and brings order; also, clear quartz's trigonal structure affects us with a balancing matrix that promotes clarity and neutrality, improving our perception and understanding of the environment. This crystal sheds light on our path and direction in life, helping us to reconnect with our deepest essence and to see our inner selves clearly. Thanks to the important presence of silicon, it directs information to our system and renders the fascial tissues supple, thus supporting the interconnection and ability to open us to life in all its forms. Try to meditate while holding a hyaline quartz in your hands; imagine that your body can gradually assume the crystal's qualities of transparency, balance and purity. When your whole body is crystal clear, imagine yourself being crossed by light and projecting it toward your dreams.

CHAPTER 4.2

PRACTICES FOR BALANCING PERSONAL AND ENVIRONMENTAL ENERGIES

Because you are inseparable from the web of life
that surrounds you, your inner work
and your caring for yourself naturally
contributes to the healing of the world.

(Rachael Wooten, American Jungian analyst,
spiritual practitioner and author)

Chapter 4.2

Start with the Soles of the Feet

The body's legs and feet represent the element of earth: they support us, maintain our balance, they are our roots.

The stronger, more flexible and stable they are, the more we'll be able to flow smoothly through life, get our bearings and elevate ourselves. Providing your feet with loving care and awareness will greatly improve your well-being. Begin by standing, keeping your knees soft and your back straight; place the sole of your foot on a tennis ball or a hard rubber ball, or even one of those trigger point massage balls. Run the ball along the entire sole, back and forth, including the toes and heel; if you come across a tender spot, run over it several times. When the sole of the foot is truly awake, warm and activated, pause and notice the difference between the two feet, then begin treating the other one the same way. One foot at a time, press the back of the toes against the ground, stretching the back of the foot and the ankle, followed by the top of the toes and lifting the heel as much as possible, putting some weight onto the toes to stretch them. Then place both feet on the ground and press the back of the toes and the heels downward, feeling how the arches lift and the leg muscles become activated and strengthened. Take a few moments to acknowledge the renewed feeling of stability and awareness of your extremities.

Finish by massaging one foot at a time, maybe using a few drops of a grounding essential oil such as vetiver, cedarwood or cypress diluted in a carrier oil. Use both hands to open and soften the sole, then focus on one toe at a time.

Now all you have to do is get up and go out into the world, aware of your every step.

Chapter 4.2

Ground Yourself with a Tree

Trees are loaded with life force: they absorb and transform earth energy from the ground and capture the cosmic forces from the sky. They are like pillars that penetrate the heavenly and earthly realms to create a bridge. Their branches stretch out toward the stars, the gods and spirits, while their roots sink into the darkness of the earth where the ancestors rest. Like trees, we also occupy a place between the two worlds, which can meet in our heart space, where a horizontal plane is created allowing us to engage. Trees have embodied this union of high and low for much longer than we have; they can teach us a great deal about integrity and the possibility of integrating the binary without succumbing to separation, honoring all aspects of ourselves and existence.

When you approach a tree, look at it with an open mind, grasping its entirety. Approach it slowly, trying to feel the full vitality of each branch, leaf or bud and viewing it as a large antenna in constant harmony with the environment. Standing or sitting, establish a connection by resting your back against the tree trunk, close your eyes and begin breathing deeply in this proximity, expanding the rib cage toward the tree trunk and perceiving this contact in its entirety. Feel your verticality connecting you from the earth to the celestial space, expand your perceptual feelers, like invisible branches, and when you feel an inner "yes," stop in the heart space, where descending and ascending energies meet. Expand this space horizontally, like a bubble, and include the tree in it to create a place for communion and listening that will give you vitality and a deep sense of belonging.

Chapter 4.2

Water Has Memory

Since the 1990s, some scholars have been talking about the memory of water, referring to water's ability to store information and vibrations coming from the environment, both in terms of actual substances as well as thoughts, words, music and images. The most significant research is that of Masaru Emoto, who conducted numerous experiments to demonstrate the ability of water to store and absorb the influences to which it is exposed. First, he put the water in contact with different external stimuli, such as words written on sheets of paper, music and prayers, then he froze it and photographed the ice crystals that formed.

The crystals exposed to kind words or harmonious music presented pleasant and orderly geometric structures, while those generated by offensive words or discordant music were jumbled and discordant.

Despite attracting much criticism, such theories have great resonance beyond the scientific field; from a holistic viewpoint, the concept that water can "remember" and respond to human intentions has garnered much renewed awareness, especially if we consider that humans are about 60% water. You may attempt to inform your drinking water by labeling it with empowering words, exposing it to music or crystals (be sure they are safe and don't contain heavy metals) by immersing them or placing them around a jug full of water; above all, you should nurture your inner waters in the knowledge they have memory. How do you talk to yourself? What messages do you wish to imprint in you?

“

Vibration is what
makes the existence
of all things possible.
Everything that exists
is in a state of vibration,
which is the source of the power.

(Masaru Emoto,
Japanese researcher and author)

”

Chapter 4.2

Boost Your Defenses with Fire Cider

Fire cider is a natural remedy created in the 1970s by American herbalist Rosemary Gladstar, inspired by folk wisdom and other herbalists, and it's well known in Anglo-Saxon countries.

This tonic has great benefits for the immune system and the circulation. It support us in the colder months and has expectorant and anti-inflammatory properties, while also being a healthy supplement in case of diabetes and cardiovascular disease. Besides being effective in preventing illness during flu season, it also has an excellent aromatic taste and can be incorporated into the diet to supply many healthy nutrients used as a dressing for salads and vegetables. The plants used in this herbal remedy are a concentrate with stimulating, antibacterial and immunostimulant properties.

Prepare in autumn and, to reap the benefits, ingest 1–2 teaspoons a day throughout the winter, ingesting it on its own, in food or diluting it in hot water or herbal tea. If you have a cold or a sore throat, you can double or triple the dose.

2 cups (1/2 l) of unpasteurized organic apple cider vinegar – 2 inches (5 cm) of ginger root cut into small pieces or grated – 1 sliced onion – 1 organic lemon peel – 2 sprigs of rosemary (approximately 4 inches/ 10 cm) – 5 sprigs of thyme – 1 tbsp of turmeric powder or 1 1/2 inches (4 cm) of fresh grated root – 10 peeled and crushed garlic cloves – 2 hot chilies. Optional: 1 sprig of yarrow, chaga mushroom powder – 4 bay leaves – 1 tsp cinnamon – 4–5 cloves, rose hip, horseradish, elderberry, nettle

Place all the ingredients in a large glass jar, seal tightly and let stand for at least four weeks, strain through a muslin cloth or use a drip coffee bag, add honey to taste and store inside a dark glass bottle.

The Great Mother

To understand the Great Mother or Mother Goddess cult, we must go back to ancient times, to the origins of first attempting to answer the questions: Where do we come from? How does what surrounds us come about?

Through archaeological findings of statuettes with bodies depicting pronounced feminine attributes, painted vulvas, vaginas and swollen breasts or rock paintings of pregnant and lactating goddesses, we know that from 30,000 BC until at least 3,000 BC, mankind worshipped a Mother Earth goddess.

She embodies the unity of all natural things: that which lives and dies, what changes and transforms, every creature and all that belongs to the goddess's great cosmic womb, from which everything is born and to which everything returns. The Great Mother represents fertility, motherhood, healing, wisdom and the creative power of nature. She's associated with the moon, water and earth, and symbolizes the cycle of life, death and rebirth. In Andean mythology, she is known as Pachamama, which in the Quechua language means "mother space time" or "mother universe," while among First Australians she is known as Kunapipi, or "uterus."

She reminds us that our origin is linked to the unity and interconnectedness of all that is, reminding us that, first of all, we are and always will be children.

FOCUS

CHAPTER 4.3

CREATING CUSTOM RITUALS TO SUPPORT WHOLESOME WELLNESS

Every fruit
clings to the seed like a pledge.
In falling, it pledges and, in the form of a root responds
to the earth that calls. To the earth that sings
the infinite promise.

(Mariangela Gualtieri, Italian poet and writer)

Chapter 4.3

Bless Your Food

Blessing the food you are about to eat is a powerful way to connect with all the beings who contributed to grow, cook and serve what you eat. It's a gesture through which we can acknowledge and give thanks, remembering that we're part of the food chain and an ecosystem, that all our actions have an impact and effect, and that we nourish ourselves on the lives of other beings, whatever our food choices. Eating is a magical act in which we transform what was other than us into a part of us; we assimilate it and take on its vitality.

What is on our plate has a story; there was a time when someone planted seeds in the ground and the rain watered them so they would sprout, then the sun fed them and made them grow, and when the fruit was ripe, someone harvested it with their hands and labor. If you eat animal products, remember that you are nourishing yourself off the life of sentient beings; this is an enormous gift that should be honored and never taken for granted. Give thanks to those who cooked using the raw materials to create uniquely magic flavors and textures. Pause before this marvel and take time to retrace the journey that the food has made to your plate. Observe the dish, inhale its aromas and take in the colors so you can be present for what you're about to do: nourish yourself.

Remember that through this practice, we celebrate our connection with all that is alive, the elemental forces and the earth's body. Always celebrate our planet's abundance and prosperity, the fruits of which sustain life. Honor is part of the cycle of life.

Chapter 4.3

The Ritual of Harvest

Whenever you go out foraging for plants, whether it's to make a concoction or to decorate the home with a nice bunch of flowers, experience the moment as if it were a gift.

Plants don't belong to you. Even if you grow them, if you have a deep connection to them and you feel like the custodian of the plant world, they are never your property.

Before harvesting them, always take the time to notice the surroundings; see what plants grow there and how they are organized, so that your act of harvesting will have the least impact on that ecosystem's unique balance. Should a plant strike you for its beauty or because of how and where it grows, leave it where it is and find another plant to pick. Leave each location as beautiful and pristine as you found it. Never take the first plant you see, as it could be the only one. Wise women recommend passing at least seven specimens before beginning to pick. Also, spend some time with the plant, participate in its life before taking part of it, listen to the being before you and be fully present in your action, like in a ceremony. Encounter the plant like a human being, not a thing to be appropriated.

At most, pick 25% of the specimens, both to leave some for others and because when you pick a flower you are interfering with its life cycle, meaning no berries or fruit will be produced, so there will be fewer seeds to support local populations. Finally, before picking a plant, ask for permission. It may seem strange, but try it: if the plant doesn't want to be picked, it will let you know.

"

Talking to plants
is a way of talking
directly to the Spirit.

(Rosemary Gladstar, American herbalist,
author and educator)

"

Chapter 4.3

Nurture the Community

We are social beings accustomed from time immemorial to living in communities and interacting; our ancestors congregated in circles around a fire or under the full moon to celebrate seasonal cycles and rites of passage.

They lived together sharing time and experiences, practicing reciprocal care. When you are sharing a beautiful moment with your loved ones, when you feel the strong connection nurturing the bonds and your soul, you are walking in the footsteps of those who came before you. You're remembering what we need as social beings. Oxytocin, released by the pituitary gland, is the hormone of love. Its essence is what you feel when you share a meal with friends and family, the beauty of singing together, or when you hold hands gazing into the eyes of the person you love. The hormone is produced during labor to allow the mother to bond with the newborn; it's also released when we establish bonds and feel happy in the company of others, or when we make love, establishing a joyful feeling of giving and receiving. It's the hormone of community and intimacy; its production shouldn't be limited to exchanges with a single person, but should include the various relationships that are part of our lives. Oxytocin balances the stress hormones like cortisol, lowering inflammation and improving the way we feel. Sharing and nurturing a community is important because it's part of our nature, it makes us feel good and helps overcome the sense of isolation we often experience nowadays that many interactions are virtual. How can you nurture and foster community? How do you feel about reinstating the habit of regular encounters with loved ones, to nurture relationships and cure loneliness?

Chapter 4.3

The Cure of Reciprocity

In most indigenous cultures, there is a sense of reciprocity with the earth; many traditions have rituals exclusively devoted to offerings, in which the celebrants donate objects, food and prayers as a means of giving thanks for everything they receive every day.

Pago a la Tierra is a well-known ceremony in the Inca tradition, which is kept alive by the Peruvian shamans in the mountains around Cuzco; its purpose is to balance reciprocity and remind us that we are "one," without separation. The act of giving creates energy and allows you to enter the flow of exchange and mutual benefit, giving gratitude, love, nurturing or a service back to the environment. Above all, such an act will make you feel positive; it will rebalance your inner self and your perception of giving and receiving. You can take concrete action by reducing waste, considering your food sources, supporting environmental causes you believe in, including poetic, spontaneous acts that will give you a strong sense of belonging to the natural world. When you go for a walk outdoors, you may take a bag with you to collect the litter you find, clearing a path or cutting a dead branch to somehow take care of the environment that has welcomed you. You may prepare a mixture of rice or other grains, seeds, rose petals, berries and nuts as an offering for wildlife, or even prepare some seed bombs, i.e., guerrilla gardening "weapons" to be thrown into city parks and vacant lots to plant vegetation in support of pollinators like bees.

6 TBSP OF ORGANIC SOIL – 4 TBSP OF POWDERED CLAY – 1 TSP OF NATIVE WILDFLOWER SEEDS (CALENDULA, THYME, LAVENDER, LACY PHACELIA, BORAGE, MALLOW, MARIGOLD, SUNFLOWER, POPPY, CORNFLOWER, ETC.) – WATER

Mix the dirt and the seeds, then add the clay, mixing everything well. Add the water a little at a time, until you obtain a malleable dough that's not overly moist, then make some balls the size of a walnut and let them dry for 2–3 days on a sheet of newspaper. Your bombs can be simply placed on the ground and watered with a bit of water on very hot days.

Bees

For the ancient Egyptians, the bee had a divine origin, having been born from the tears of Ra, and was seen as part of the soul, capable of bringing the dead back to life by entering their mouths. Bees are also part of the Great Mother goddess cult. During the Eleusinian Mysteries, some rites required the mouth and hands to be washed with honey, to signify the purification of words and deeds, while the priestesses were called "melissae" or "friends of the bees." The bee symbolizes community as it cannot live alone, but exclusively in the hive, which is a single entity and a super organism. A bee is born, grows and dies, but the hive is eternal and inside it lies the queen bee, the only fertile female tasked with generating the eggs that will produce the new members of the community, specifically, the worker bees. It's they who produce the honey, a golden elixir made from the nectar of many different flowers, which reminds us that sweetness is the fruit of the gifts of the earth, when they are grown with care and devotion. Propolis, on the other hand, is a protective substance used in phytotherapy for its antimicrobial and healing qualities. It reminds us of the importance of healthy boundaries in life and in relationships, while the wax with which the bees build the honeycomb represents the sacred container that the community needs to grow and thrive in love.

CHAPTER 5

REBIRTH: Inner Blossoming

To rejuvenate is to be able to cross over to the end, accepting ashes like fertilizer, seeing beyond the fruiting stage and knowing that after the fullness, there must inevitably be a void, because to generate new life, a fertile space is needed. We are born and die continuously; parts of us, identities, projects and relationships die to make room for something else. The leaves fall to make room for new buds, fruits offer themselves to animals so that their seeds can be transported and delivered to the earth, where death becomes life and waste is nourishment.

In this chapter, you will learn the art of rejuvenation through the acceptance of shadows and wounds, through blessed rest and the realm of dreams, which are the breeding ground for what is new, to meet a powerful and inspired vision.

CHAPTER 5.1

FOSTERING GRATITUDE AND NURTURING THE SOUL

If the only prayer you ever say
in your entire life is "thank you,"
that will suffice.

(Meister Eckhart, German theologian, philosopher and mystic from the Christian Middle Ages)

Chapter 5.1

Appreciation, Gratitude and Eyes Full of Wonder

When you feel gratitude or express appreciation, when you tune in to the gifts you receive from someone or something, a change takes place in your inner self, from a state of lacking to one of abundance. In this state, your attention is no longer on what you lack as you focus on what you already have: in doing so, your heart's energy field becomes consistent, balanced and harmonious.

This may be challenging, given our habit of focusing on what is missing and the negative facets of our lives, due to cultural and environmental conditioning, traumatic experiences and unconscious behaviors. Nonetheless, we can all choose to consciously ignore our conditioning and come up with new ways of being that are more empowering and improve our lives.

To rewire your attitude and acquire a new outlook on things, it's important that you give yourself some time for a simple daily practice: start the day with two minutes of gratitude for the miracle of being alive and for all the joy that life gives you. You may even make a list of things you appreciate in your life and, where there are or were tricky situations, try and see if the problem may be concealing a gift you may have overlooked.

Before going to sleep, you could chat with those you live with and share what you appreciated about them during the day, or you may do this with yourself, pausing to appreciate some of your actions, thoughts and attitudes. Try to embody and practice gratitude by focusing on the present and looking at the world with eyes full of wonder.

Chapter 5.1

Rest Is Revolutionary

We live in a world that demands we be productive, that pressures and exhausts us, in a culture that expects us to always be busy and filled with things to do, in which resting is a form of laziness. And so, we feel guilty if we take a vacation, pushing ourselves beyond our capabilities and our limits, ignoring the body, blaming ourselves for not being productive even when we're going through something challenging.

The original vision of rest is connected to the ancestral heartbeat; it's a very important phase of rejuvenation. Rest is medicine; it's a right and a physiological necessity. Even the earth has its downtime, winter, in which everything is still and suspended, when life is gestated through rest. Likewise, we need to recharge by walking through meadows and woodlands, along streams, rivers and beaches, listening to birdsong, watching the coming and going of bees loaded with pollen, or the fluttering of butterflies and dragonflies. We are recharged by lying in a mountain meadow, glaring at the buzzards circling in the clear sky and enjoying the coolness beneath the foliage. We rejuvenate by learning to establish boundaries and protect our personal time and space, making room for introspection, meditation, prayer and gratitude. We recharge by sleeping and taking conscious naps when we need to. By resting, we practice being inactive and nurture the feeling of being enough, we defuse competitiveness, self-criticism and the ongoing feelings of struggle and fatigue, reconnecting to the source of creativity, of ease and flow.

Chapter 5.1

Nurturing the Soul Through Healing Stories

Stories make us human; they inspire us and have the power to change the world. A story can be healing, loving, freeing.

Shamans of all ethnicities and traditions use "healing stories" to unblock people in tricky situations into a liberating perspective using the poetry of words, which build worlds and create opportunities. Healing stories are comprised of creative images, words that trigger radical transformative processes in us. These are stories that speak to the soul and are universal, despite each drawing on its own mythological tradition and vision of the cosmos.

When a healing story is told, each listener will hear a different story; each one will grasp exactly what they need at the exact time they hear it. The healing narrative leads us to a positive change and a broader vision of ourselves and the world; it should not be understood with the mind, but rather, experienced through the body and the senses, relying on its ability to shape and transform our perception of the world and, thus, the world itself.

Storytelling as medicine presumes that we are ourselves the story and that the way we live depends very much on the story we tell ourselves. Our future comes from our past, which shapes how we live and feel; however, it's a past that is nonetheless the result of a subjective narrative. Changing this way of narrating ourselves means transforming the past and being open to new opportunities, it means activating powerful healing powers within us. What story are you telling yourself and what story would you like to tell yourself?

I am never stagnant;
I rise from my worst disasters,
I turn, I change.

(Virginia Woolf, British writer,
essayist and activist)

Chapter 5.1

Make Room for Your Heart

There are times in life and throughout the year when we may feel melancholy, have a heavy heart or are emotionally tired, all of which disconnect us from the feeling of joy. Sometimes this happens at the end of winter, when the lack of daylight has long prevailed and the cold around us has seeped into our bones. When you feel disconnected from life, from joy and love, when you feel disheartened or bitter, try honoring your heart by listening to its truth, without wanting to escape any complex feelings or discomfort, but being present like a quiet witness who watches compassionately and gently welcomes what occurs within you, without attachment or wanting to mentalize what happens. When you are able to be present like this, for yourself at difficult times, and when you are able to sit with uncomfortable emotions and sadness in your heart, you are doing something major for yourself.

You are appealing to the possibility within you that is greater than yourself.

You are open to vulnerability that can be turned into a resource.

Plants teach us to remain upright and grounded during a storm, to trust in the sun's return, the coming rains, the ripening of fruit.

This recipe will nourish your heart, warming it and giving it the hug it needs. Like a loving mother, cocoa will cradle you in its arms, the rose with its soft petals will soothe and heal your wounds, cinnamon will ignite your passion and activate your energy, vanilla will give you sweetness and support.

You can prepare it as follows:

1 organic vanilla pod – 1 cinnamon stick – 1 handful of Damask rose buds – 1/2 cup (50 g) of raw cocoa – 2 cups (500 ml) of rum or brandy

Crumble all the ingredients or crush them in a mortar, then pour them into a large, clean glass jar and pour in the rum or brandy. Screw on the cap and let it rest in the dark for two months, shaking the jar every day.

Strain with a piece of gauze or a drip coffee bag, add honey as needed and transfer everything to a dark glass bottle.

You may have a spoonful, even diluted in boiling water to evaporate the alcohol, whenever you wish to give your heart warmth and acceptance.

Cocoa

— THEOBROMA CACAO

Native to Central America, this seed is contained in the orange-red fruit of a tropical evergreen tree. For thousands of years, it was considered the "food of the gods" and revered as a sacred plant; nowadays, it's widely consumed in every part of the world for its delicious flavor and beneficial properties. It's great for the circulation and nervous system, promoting heart health and lowering blood pressure; it provides energy and is rich in minerals, encouraging joy and uplifting the spirit.

It's a plant that bolsters the sense of being grounded, helps one relax and awakens a sense of happiness and euphoria, increasing motivation, mental clarity and the spontaneous creativity that springs from happiness and pleasure.

It has aphrodisiac properties and promotes the opening of the heart and connecting with others; its essence contains maternal qualities, seductiveness and wise loving kindness; it prompts us to explore and radiate infinite forms of love, keeping them together. It takes us on a deep journey into the heart of life, reconnecting us to beauty, gentleness and love for ourselves and others, healing emotional wounds, fostering forgiveness and inviting us to release attachments.

CHAPTER 5.2

A JOURNAL OF MAGIC TO RECORD ONE'S JOURNEY

Does this street have a heart?
Is the only question that matters.
If it does, it's a good street.
If it doesn't, it should be discarded.

(Carlos Castaneda, Peruvian writer and anthropologist, naturalized US citizen)

Chapter 5.2

The Dream World as a Guide

In ancient times, dreams were considered prophetic and were examined for divinatory purposes; there were spaces devoted to "incubating a dream," that is, receiving a revelation from the dream.

Anthropologist Kilton Stewart, who in 1935 spent a year among the Malaysian tribe of the Senoi, noted how the children of these people were given a proper education in dreaming. He explained that to face and conquer the common fears that occur in dreams, one must regard them as the expression of latent energies asking to be integrated into one's personality. The dream always comes to the rescue, providing powerful imagery; it reveals important transitions and can show us that upsetting characters or emotions may actually conceal allies trying to reach out to us. A dream doesn't speak rationally or logically; the images in dreams appear as a riddle with a symbolic meaning that mustn't be deciphered, but understood and appreciated within us.

The main purpose of working with dreams is to re-establish a natural way to contact one's deeper self. This occurs through the messages of the instinct and the collective unconscious, and thanks to the infinite creative opportunities arising in dreams, all of which facilitate the decoding process or, according to Carl Jung, the path where an individual becomes increasingly aware of their unconscious traits and integrates them into their consciousness. If you are intrigued by this practice, start keeping a dream diary that you should always keep at your bedside, so you can jot down your dreams as soon as you wake up, before they fade away. Writing is a tool that will help you decipher the dream-like sensations and impressions by bringing them into consciousness.

Chapter 5.2

Dreaming with Herbs

Dream pillows are as old as time and have been used for centuries to aid sleep. Today they're still popular, providing a fragrant and comforting way to drift into Morpheus's arms. Herbs are masters at ferrying us into dreamland and their vibrations are very close to the liminal states of consciousness, such as hypnagogia, the transitional phase between wakefulness and sleep, or hypnopompia, the state when we awake from sleep. Sleeping with herbs is also a wonderful way to get to know them, absorbing their properties and discovering their mysteries!

A dream pillow can be carefully handmade, embroidered with the moon and stars, made of soft velvet and decorated with lace or fringes, or it can be a simple ready-made cotton bag, depending on individual tastes and skills. The important thing is to choose natural fibers such as organic cotton, silk, hemp or linen.

The blends of herbs you can place inside are endless, like the dreams they will inspire. Even a single herb is enough to reap powerful effects. You may even choose to add a few drops of essential oil that matches the basic mixture, though this is optional.

2 PARTS LAVENDER – 2 PARTS ROSE PETALS –
1 PART MUGWORT – 1 PART CHAMOMILE – 1 PART BLUE LOTUS –
1/2 PART HOPS – 1/2 PART ROSEMARY
OPTIONAL: 5 DROPS OF LAVENDER,
ROSE OR CHAMOMILE ESSENTIAL OIL

Get or make a cloth bag that is approximately between 4x4 inches and 8x8 inches, but feel free to make different shapes you find inspiring and decorate it to your liking. Leave an opening that you will close later, so you can add the herbs. Blend the carefully dried herbs in a bowl and place them inside the bag, with the help of a funnel if needed, then close the seam to keep the herbs inside. Place it beside your pillow and lightly fluff it up before falling asleep to release the herbs' aroma and energy.

Chapter 5.2

Integrating the Shadow

Carl Jung, founder of analytical psychology, spoke of the shadow as a "dark and unknown side of one's personality," a realm that contains all the aspects that are not accepted or integrated by our consciousness. Often, it's we who force parts of ourselves we don't accept into a psychic prison, until these repressed forces start to emerge, sometimes even violently and unexpectedly. Fear may cause us to use even more personal energy to cast these "demons" back into the shadow, thus their power will become even more unpredictable and controlling. What lives in the shadows is actually just a force asking to be seen, accepted and embraced. These are often wounded parts, traumas that we consider unlovable and shameful, parts that are still raw, unruly and immature. What we relegate to the shadow only gains more strength, but awareness and acceptance can liberate us from this threat. Lama Tsultrim Allione, with regard to the Tibetan practice of chöd, notes that the more we fight our shadow the stronger it becomes; if we want to rid ourselves of it, rather than opposing it, we must nurture it. This way, all the pent up energy trapped in the shadow can turn into an allied force, and the demon becomes a protector.

There are practices and traditions that show us how, by connecting with the shadow, we can be reborn in freedom and with new powers. Like digging in the dark soil and finding a gold nugget, our gifts await. Right behind a dense and deep shadow, behind an uncontrolled, wild force, there is a bright light of immense wealth.

The shadow is the greatest teacher
for how to come to the light.

(Ram Dass, American psychologist and mystic)

Chapter 5.2

The Soul's Song

Each whale sings an individual song without ever repeating the same pattern: like the whales, each of us has a personal note and sings a unique song that can enrich and elevate us collectively.

From their wisdom, you can learn to express what is uniquely yours, your song, your one-of-a-kind gift to offer the world.

Your voice is unique, and so is your soul's song.

Your voice has a power that transcends the boundaries of space and time; it can inspire, excite and create waves of change that reverberate in the lives of others. Embracing it requires courage, it means stepping out of the shadow and renouncing the safety of conformity and accepting the vulnerability of revealing oneself. It means recognizing yourself, accepting yourself, writing your own story, showing yourself by overcoming the fear of judgment that dwells within you. Learn to listen to your voice; explore your values, beliefs and passions with open curiosity. Reflect on your life's journey, the challenges you've overcome and the lessons you've learned. Embrace the richness of your experiences, because they gave your voice an authentic and unique power.

Once you've connected with your uniqueness, share it fearlessly. Write, speak, sing, create: express yourself in ways that resonate with your soul. Learn to listen to the voices of others without conforming and without overpowering them, learn to nurture human harmony and create bridges, contributing your own unique melody. Take responsibility for what you say and convey. If you are authentic, you will reach hearts and inspire others to find their souls' songs as well.

Eagle

The eagle is a symbol of power and vision; it teaches us to soar, to explore the vast sky, to find new perspectives. It symbolizes the spiritual warrior, prompting us to open our eyes and gain greater clarity, to tune into the deepest truth at the heart of a situation. It's the spirit of the air, the undisputed ruler of infinity, an emblem of the higher self that breathes inspiration into us. The man that turns into an eagle is a traditional image of various shamanic traditions: the spirit frees itself from material constraints to start seeing reality differently. Distancing oneself from things presents them in a different light, and detachment merges with surprise. The flight of the eagle is a journey into the heavens, where the immense spaces speak to the infinity of our soul, capable of embracing things in their totality. It's a descent toward the earth, to translate this breadth into reality and action.

It's in the balance of heaven and earth that the eagle brings its medicine, able to soar and get close to the sun's fire more than any other animal, yet also capable of diving down to the ground, straight toward what it needs to feed and live.

CHAPTER 5.3

PREPARING FOR THE FUTURE WITH RENEWED AWARENESS

What I want is for everything to be circular and kind of not to be there, no beginning nor end of form, but rather for it to give the idea of a harmonious whole, that of life.

(Vincent Van Gogh, Dutch post-impressionist painter, one of the greatest artists of all time)

Chapter 5.3

There Is No Wound That Cannot Be Healed by Love

(Robin Wall Kimmerer, Potawatomi forest biologist, academic and writer)

In Japanese spiritual philosophy, kintsugi is the art of repairing broken objects with gold. It's said that kintsugi may have originated in the 15th century under shogun Ashikaga Yoshimasa; it reminds us that we can turn our physical and emotional wounds into opportunities and sources of strength. Healing, therefore, is not returning to a state preceding the rupture, but the opportunity to expose a mental or physical wound to a mending that makes it precious. Thus, all the cracks become visible through the gold joinery, adding even more value to the object.

In our culture, we're accustomed to discarding or neglecting that which is damaged, while revering what is new and flawless; however, the lesson behind this technique is to trust in life, blessing any wounds as unavoidable changes that enrich us.

The suffering that urges you to wander into the dark night of the soul is not intended to cause you pain, but to lead you to discover something that is not yet clear. Thus, the scar turns into a bright window through which to filter perception and see something new.

Kintsugi is comparable to the inner alchemy described by Carl Jung: from the nigredo stage, in which we are forced to let go of our broken parts, we transition to the albedo stage, which is the process of repairing, sanding, gluing and applying gold dust. This second stage constitutes an actual rebirth; it's the start of a new, empowering life. The third stage, called rubedo, is when new matter is created that surpasses the sum of the materials and the process.

Chapter 5.3

Listen to Your Inner Power

There's a part of you acting as your compass, pointing you in the right direction and guiding your decision making. And no, it's not the mind. To make decisions, you don't need to think and evaluate, assess risks and benefits or be strategic. The mind is never in the present moment, it's always in the past, recollecting past experiences, or in the future, anticipating anxieties about what could happen. The mind is a wonderful instrument when used for what it's designed to do, namely, comparing experiences, mastering systems, learning and re-examining; however, it's inadequate for decision making.

The latter must take place in the body, which is alive, intelligent, sensitive, attuned to the present and safety and evolution oriented. That's why the important decisions must be "felt" in the body, in its wisdom and its wonderful ability to guide us—if we let it—especially if it's clean, free from having to be and having to do what doesn't relate to us, and heard. No one knows what's good for you better than you; no one has your sensitivity and your energetic system. We are at a time when, as human beings, we have evolved to the point of being able to leave aside external powers, leaders and gurus; we have the tools of self-knowledge, like Human Design, which take us back to our center, our inner home, recognizing and freeing ourselves from conformity, embracing our unique nature and experiencing it fully. Human Design guides you to discover what part of yourself you should tune in to: your emotions, your gut, your intuition, your willpower, your voice as you talk about it, your connection to the moon. It asks you to consider what is right for you.

“

And what we're here to express
is that quality of uniqueness
that differentiates us
from everyone else.

(Ra Uru Hu, founder and messenger
of the Human Design System)

”

Chapter 5.3

Gracefully Embracing the Passage of Time

Taoism sees aging as a natural part of life, a process to be embraced rather than rejected.

The Taoist philosophy has a deep understanding of the natural cycles, and aging is seen as a reflection of these cycles, not something to be feared or fought, but rather, an opportunity for personal growth and spiritual development. By embracing the wisdom that comes with age, we can access a deeper understanding of ourselves and the world around us. The underlying vision is that our growth is always an evolutionary path; if nature diminishes our strength and physical prowess, in exchange it gives us added vision and wisdom. As we age, we gain a wealth of knowledge and experiences that can guide us in making wiser decisions and living more authentically. With age comes a wider perspective, a deeper understanding of what really matters in life.

By embracing the wisdom of age, we can let go of the need for external affirmation and focus more on living in line with our values and desires. Of course, in order to age gracefully, a healthy lifestyle with adequate exercise, nutrition and meditation, as well as conscious rest, are all essential. There are also many important plants, such as sea buckthorn, rich in antioxidants and fatty acids; *Ginkgo biloba* and *Centella asiatica*, which promote brain function and microcirculation; ginseng, which increases vitality and energy; and astragalus, which supports a healthy heart. Above all, let's accept the passage of time as an evolutionary process that nature has designed for us.

Chapter 5.3

Make Your Own Incense for an Emotional Journey

Our sense of smell is a powerful associative tool. Smell bypasses our brain's verbal centers and connects us directly to memories and emotions; a smell can awaken memories at a visceral level through the emotional hook. That's why, if we commit to intentionally using our sense of smell, we can create positive and beneficial associations. A beautiful way to do this is to create a homemade incense blend to burn whenever you feel the need, combining scents and aromas that awaken memories to warm your heart and uplift your spirit. The base of an incense mixture is resin that's produced by the healing wounds of trees; it's like aromatic gold that flows from the healing of our experiences. We can buy resins such as myrrh, copal or frankincense, but let's not forget that we can also collect the resin of trees directly from the woods, especially from conifers. Their healing aroma soothes and clears the lungs, prompting us to embrace life more. Do not remove all the resin from the tree wound and pick the harder bits, not the sticky ones.

To make it even harder and easier to work with a pestle, put it in the freezer for a few hours.

– Herbs: use dried, ground herbs in about half the mixture. Try to include a variety of bitter and sweet herbs or roots. Among the bitter herbs you can use mugwort, yarrow leaves, juniper berries, wormwood, cypress, rosemary and thyme. Among the sweet herbs choose rose petals, lavender, yarrow flowers, elderflowers, fir needles, cinnamon and citrus peels.

– Resin: for the other half of the concoction, use a pestle to pulverize the resin.

Put the ingredients in a jar and mix well, adding a few drops of essential oil if needed. When you feel like burning some, in a bowl with a little sand or an incense burner, light a bit of charcoal and let it burn for half a minute. Then add some mixture, relax your nostrils and let the scent guide you on a beautiful journey through feelings and memories.

Dhumavati

Dhumavati is a Tantric goddess, depicted as an elderly woman who accompanies all moments of mourning, death and going through pain. She's the big void and we have much to learn from her.

She's depicted on a stationary cart, with a thin and shriveled body that represents the time that has already passed, holding a sieve with which she separates the wheat from the chaff, as she embodies the truth that is acquired over time, from having lived through all the stages of life and knowing how to discern between what we want to pass on to those who will come after us and what should be forgotten. Once the fruit is eaten, the seed remains, which contains all the instructions to grow a new tree; it's from the seed that life begins again. Dhumavati is the Divine Mother who has become old, she is smoky and evanescent and is often worshipped at cremation grounds. She's disappearing, preparing to become an ancestor and return to the earth to make room for a new life. She's with us during the death of some parts of us, through rites of passage. She teaches us to let go and dissipate without attachment. Dying is also part of life, after all, we begin to die the moment we are born. The awareness of departing and of what we leave behind, is her great gift.

FOCUS

Anastasia Mostacci

Since childhood, Anastasia Mostacci has nurtured a great interest in visible and invisible connections. She has studied philosophy and yoga while simultaneously dedicating herself to the study of plants: learning to identify them, listening to their subtle voices, eating them and making remedies. Since 2015, she has been working on projects and ventures aimed at fostering communication between human beings and nature. Accompanied by the spirits of plants, she guides evolutionary journeys focused on the knowledge of and the relationship with the plant world.

Sara Marcuzzi

Sara Marcuzzi is an illustrator who studied advertising design and photography. After a start using watercolors, in 2018 she ventured into digital art. For her, art is a means of giving a voice to hidden emotions.